# Strategies and Tactics in Fashion Marketing

## SELECTED READINGS

**SIDNEY PACKARD**

FAIRCHILD PUBLICATIONS · NEW YORK

Designed by Karen Wiedman

Copyright © 1982 by Fairchild Publications
Division of Capital Cities Media, Inc.

Permission has been granted to reprint
previously published articles.

Standard Book Number: 87005-410-4

Library of Congress Catalog Card Number: 82-70063

Printed in the United States of America

# Table of Contents

**INTRODUCTION** ............................................................ v

**SECTION ONE—FASHION MARKETING CONCEPTS** ............................................................ 1

  1. Marketing and Its Application to Apparel Producers
    *Knitting Times,* official publication of the National Knitwear and Sportswear Association, April 1979.... 1

  2. Planning A Marketing Program: Where to Begin
    *Knitting Times,* November 1979 ............................... 8

  3. Planning A Retail Distribution System
    *Knitting Times,* August 1979 ................................. 12

  4. Selling—A Marketing Activity
    Chapter 1 of a book in the planning stage with the working title of *Concepts and Cases For Applied Personal Selling* .................................................. 16

**SECTION TWO—PLANNING** ............................................. 25

  5. How to Assess Consumer Buying Power
    *Knitting Times,* February 1980 ................................ 26

  6. Consumer Buying Power
    *Apparel World,* official publication of the National Knitwear and Sportswear Association, March 1980 ......... 30

  7. Merchandising By Classification
    *Apparel World,* May 1981 ...................................... 32

  8. Consumer Research
    Chapter 2, *Consumer Behavior and Fashion Marketing,* 2nd Edition, Wm. C. Brown, 1979 ........ 37

  9. Income and Expenditure
    Chapter 4, *Consumer Behavior and Fashion Marketing,* 2nd Edition, Wm. C. Brown, 1979 ........ 50

  10. Location
    Chapter 3, *Start Your Own Store,* Prentice-Hall, 1982 ................................................................. 61

**SECTION THREE—SELLING: SALES PROMOTION** ............................................................ 69

  11. Opportunities Through Sales Promotion
    *Knitting Times,* January 1980 ................................. 69

*Strategies and Tactics in Fashion Marketing*

12. Sales Promotion
 *Concepts and Cases in Fashion Buying and Merchandising,* Fairchild Publications, 1977 ............. 74
13. What Makes A Successful Road Sales Force and How to Build One
 *Knitting Times,* May 1980 ............................................. 81
14. Non-Store Retailing: A New Apparel Opportunity
 *Apparel World,* January 1981 ................................. 86
15. Using Co-Operative Advertising Money
 *Knitting Times,* September 1981 ............................. 92

## SECTION FOUR—TRENDS ............................. 97

16. Retailing and Merchandising in the Future
 Previously unpublished .................................................. 97
17. Industry Viewpoint: Alternatives for Survival
 *Knitting Times,* July 1979 ............................................ 107
18. Regional Marts' Success Draws Industry Away From New York
 *Apparel World,* November 1980 ............................. 109
19. The Import Syndrome and Apparel Marketing
 *Apparel World,* May 1980 ......................................... 113
20. Understanding the "Jean Phenomenon"
 *Apparel World,* March 1981 ...................................... 118
21. President Reagan's Options to Aid Business: An Interpretation
 Previously unpublished .................................................. 121
22. The Maturation of Branch Stores
 *Apparel World,* April 1981 ......................................... 124
23. Fashion Marketing Implications of the 1980 Census
 *Apparel World,* July 1981 ........................................... 129

# Introduction

THE FASHION APPAREL business is one of the major segments of the nation's economic structure; it currently generates approximately $100 billion annually at retail. When the employees of 175,000 fashion-related stores are added to the number of workers and executives of the textile and manufacturing sectors, the figure of 2,500,000 exceeds the number of people employed by any other industry. Government (federal, state and local) is the only area that employs more people. Moreover, fashion apparel sales are the backbone of department stores and giant merchandise chains and are of increasing importance to many mail order operations, not to mention the tens of thousands apparel specialty stores.

Although apparel is a product of universal need, there is a relative scarcity of literature on the subject. There is a general lack of knowledge about its history, economic value and motivational factors that persuade customers to make purchases.

Historians are aware that the source of materials for fashion, namely the textile industry, has had a profound influence on the course of history, foreign relations; and the domestic policies of the strongest eighteenth century power—England. In addition, textile activity has been interwoven with most scientific and economic events of the past two hundred years in such areas as: advances in chemistry, the Industrial Revolution, development of the factory system, and advent of the age of computers.

Ironically, modern ready-to-wear is a relatively young industry, born in 1920. In that year a confluence of events caused the development of a new industry—mass production of "store clothing" for the mass market. The linkage included the following events:

- Manufacturers, after having utilized the factory system to produce uniforms for World War I, needed another mass market.

- With limited time to sew, females entering the commercial world needed apparel made for them—"store clothing."
- The development of rayon provided a fabric cheap enough for mass apparel.
- The population movement to urban areas established heavy concentrations of people for mass distribution.
- Movies and the automobile: the first heightened interest in fashion, the second increased sociability. Both led to increased interest in apparel.

It must be noted that the foregoing relates to women's apparel—the men's industry began in the early nineteenth century. However, it was the women's fashion industry, based on consumer acceptance, that gave impetus and importance to modern fashion marketing practices.

In the beginning, apparel producers as a group were not considered economically significant; the entrenched retailers—department store operators—did not consider ready-to-wear important as an inventory category. When, however, factory-made apparel gained wider consumer acceptance, retailers recognized its volume potential and began paying attention to fashion marketing. In the 1950's and early 1960's, Wall Street—the financial hub of the nation—acknowledged the magnitude of the ready-to-wear business by helping large-scale apparel producers to "go public"—that is, sell shares of company ownership to outside investors.

In due course, some apparel producers of men's and women's apparel became "giants," achieving yearly sales figures in the hundreds of millions of dollars. Examples include Jonathan Logan, Puritan Fashions, Warnaco, and Phillips-Van Heusen. Large conglomerates—highly diversified publicly owned corporations—as exemplified by Consolidated Foods and General Mills, entered the apparel field by acquiring apparel manufacturing firms.

Retail concentration on apparel has become intense with strong competition in most trading areas. Fashion apparel now accounts for about 52 percent of department store sales; apparel discounters have proliferated at a rapid pace, chain and specialty stores have become sophisticated outlets for fashion merchandise.

Yet, in an age of technology, manufacturers, to a significant degree, have lagged in using available technology; they still produce apparel in the time-honored way of cutting goods on a table with an electrified cutting tool, followed by an assembly line sewing process. This labor-intensive method has made the industry vulnerable to the comparative advantage of cheap labor available to foreign producers. In the years following World War II, foreign manufacturers made increasingly deeper domestic market penetration. The United States, as the world leader of mass-produced apparel, is being chal-

*Introduction*

lenged by the foreign-produced apparel, not unlike the American automobile industry, which is currently in second place in the world market, behind Japan.

Academic study of fashion apparel is confined largely to designing and merchandising (or retailing). Production is given limited consideration. Technical aspects, most business students hold, could lead to factory work, an area that is not regarded as sufficiently prestigious or rewarding. Yet, if the industry is to achieve its former level of leadership, it will have to do so by taking full advantage of American technology. The U.S. fashion industry has no other means of neutralizing the advantage of cheap labor in competing nations.

The selected writings that follow were published during the past five years and represent the author's point of view about fashion marketing, a long-held fascination. If the material helps a fashion marketer to develop a successful strategy or tactic, or fortifies a student's decision to enter the fashion business, the author will deem his efforts worthwhile.

Grateful acknowledgment is extended to collegues who helped to make this publication possible:

Eric Hertz—Editor—Knitting Times/Apparel World
John Duhring—Editor—Prentice-Hall
William Cox—Editor—Wm. C. Brown
Joseph Miranda—Editor—Fairchild Books
Ed Gold—Manager—Fairchild Books
Arthur Winters—Co-Author—Fashion Buying and Merchandising
Nathan Axelrod—Co-Author—Fashion Buying and Merchandising
Abraham Raine—Co-Author—Consumer Behavior and Fashion Marketing

*Sidney Packard*
*Boynton Beach, Florida*
*May, 1981*

# SECTION ONE

# Fashion Marketing Concepts

EVERY BUSINESS, organized formally or informally, is a marketing structure with one goal—*to make profit.* Although no one has ever identified every marketing function, the general consensus among marketing authorities is that the categories of marketing activities are merchandising, physical distribution, and various supporting activities (see Article 1 for specifics).

Marketing includes the construction of a marketing system to respond effectively to a marketing environment. A system consists of individuals who are assigned the duties of receiving problems and/or developing marketing opportunities to achieve profit and to enhance the probability of achieving organizational goals.

The consumer approach of all marketing activities is *planning.* Business success is founded on plans that develop strategies and tactics that respond to controllable and uncontrollable environmental factors—with the primary purpose of producing consumer-satisfying products or services.

The four units in this section are concerned with the *definition* and *activities of marketing:*

Articles 1 and 2 focuses on apparel producers, but the principles and activities are also pertainable to all other sectors of the industry.

Articles 3 and 4 highlights the application of an activity of marketing—selling.

## 1. MARKETING AND ITS APPLICATIONS TO APPAREL PRODUCERS

Survival is the common concentration of apparel producers. What other business has an annual attrition rate of 17 percent? What other industry yields the greater return on capital and the lowest return on sales? How many firms of 25 years ago are still operating today?

A great idea, a highly successful season and even a fine record as a key resource for major retailers are ephemeral values; yesterday's success can be tomorrow's failure.

The fashion apparel business—the purveyors of finished goods—are indeed a class apart from most other businesses, including the textile and retail fashion sectors. The average firm is a comparatively small operation with limited capital and on the edge, but not in the mainstream of available technological developments.

"There's no business like the fashion business," is a cliché, but is there any other way to describe one that must contend with:

- Severe competition
- Strong reliance on psychological obsolescence (Do we wear out apparel?)
- Low intrinsic value relationship (jeans at $45.00?)
- Seasonality (Several hit lines in a year?)
- The condition of change that necessitates high markdowns and fast turnover.

The Horatio Alger stories of yesterday may not be relegated to the past, but the incidence of occurrence has become rare. Despite organization size and capital limitations, apparel firms have been forced to become more sophisticated in their approach to how a business should be conducted. Increasing competition, domestic and foreign, and a more knowledgeable and willful consumer demand a planned operation. Today's "ball game" is far removed from the one played yesterday by ear, when *ad hoc* decisions were made daily.

## A Planned Operation

Although the common goals of all businesses—profit, growth, and longevity—still elude many apparel firms, there is evidence that large scale retail needs of the present, more so in the future, may be the footing for some apparel producers to reach the reward plateau enjoyed by many well organized, successful business enterprises.

If a planned operation is a necessity to survive and profit, and there is virtual unanimity on this point, it is well for apparel producers to study and apply the *modus operandi* of the great number of American businesses that responded successfully to the new environmental factors that started in the 1950's.

Immediately subsequent to World War II, changes in the American environment began to take place and accelerate at an unprecedented pace. The factors are so numerous that the subject is worthy of a treatise of considerable length. For the sake of brevity, the following is a summary of highlights:

# Fashion Marketing Concepts

- Discretionary income increased by leaps and bounds.
- Higher education became widespread.
- National credit systems became a way of life.
- Technology proliferated at a rate too fast for the average consumer's comprehension.
- Conglomerate activity became a way of big business life.
- Marketing channels took on new dimensions.
- Government marketing laws and business regulations multiplied and now total 70,000 pages.
- The global market blossomed into serious competition.
- Chauvinism became the watchword for supporters of equal female rights.
- A new lifestyle emerged in the 1960's and had a profound effect on consumer's attitudes about products.

## Marketing Concentration

The response of successful businesses to these changes was the concentration on *marketing*. Marketing is not a new term, but it is currently and constantly used, and often abused. The frequency of improper usage is surprising, particularly the confusion of the difference between *marketing* and *merchandising*.

The truth is that marketing has been practiced from the day when someone produced more products than could be consumed and had to seek consumers to obtain value for their exchange. As goods were produced in greater quantities, local markets could not absorb the output, and markets beyond local areas were sought.

American industry answered the challenges of the chain of historical events by changing marketing focuses. For example, in response to the Industrial Revolution that created a seller's market (when demand exceeded supply), the thrust was to produce as much as possible and satisfy demand. In the late nineteenth and early twentieth centuries, the focus became twofold: produce more and maximize profit.

About 1920, the word "surplus" crept into the business lexicon. In some sectors, a "buyer's market" (when supply exceeds demand) developed, and caused firms to intensify their selling efforts.

By the 1960's ownership of production facilities and the ability to make goods were not sufficient reasons for commercial success. Technology had become readily available, domestically and internationally. In fact, the global market was in the age of puberty around 1950. Production levels were more than ample to fill demand. The result was still another marketing development—the philosophy of "consumer orientation"—knowing what people want, when they want it, at what price they will buy it, and in what quantities they can absorb it. This new attitude took into account that the consumer plays an active role in the marketing process, and that failure to make goods for consumer satisfaction leads to over-production and commercial loss.

The 1970's brought about still another marketing intensification in the form of "The Total Marketing Concept." This "team-spirit game" developed when executives realized that a marketing structure can be as strong as its weakest link. Every department was examined, assigned responsibilities, and challenged with the necessity to play a role that contributes to organizational objectives.

## An American Creation

Marketing is not a mysterious maze of practices that take place behind locked executive doors. Modern marketing is an American creation that evolved in the 1950's in response to the above-listed environmental changes that also included the rapid availability of business information and product sameness. Corporate profit and growth became dependent on effective marketing. The marketing functions were delegated the mission of performing those business tasks that lead to customer satisfaction and result in profit through the development and distribution of consumer-satisfying goods.

The activites of marketing are classified into three categories and nine activites:

## The Activities of Marketing

A. Merchandising Activities
 1. Product planning and development
 2. Standardizing and grading
 3. Buying and assembling
 4. Selling
B. Physical Distribution Activities
 5. Storage
 6. Transportation
C. Supporting Activities
 7. Marketing/financing
 8. Market risk bearing
 9. Obtaining and analyzing marketing information

It can be seen from this listing that marketing is the umbrella of all business activities, and that merchandising is one category of it.

The most subjective areas, the ones that contribute most to success, are numbers (1) and (9). If there is understanding of what consumers will buy (consumer orientation), and the proper products are planned, then every other step is a matter of calculation, working with figures that have specific and finite value.

It should be noted that marketing has important implications:

# Fashion Marketing Concepts

- Managerial teamwork is paramount.
- Planning is the basis of all decisions.
- Pricing concedes a competitive world.
- Communication—internally and with consumers—is a mandate.
- The consumer must be satisfied.
- Profit is the result of marketing efficiency.

The foregoing leads to the definition of the term *marketing:* "A total business interaction which includes the planning, pricing, promotion and distribution of consumer wanted goods and/or services for a corporate profit." Marketing must be concerned with proper responses to the environment, which includes forces or factors that are both controllable and uncontrollable.

## Business Hierarchy

Management is the hub from which all organizational goals emanate. It is the highest level of the business hierarachy that examines and then determines the product, the way in which it is to be sold, at what price, the manner of storage and transportation, and to whom it is to be sold. The uncontrollable factors add up to the external conditions of both the domestic and the international areas.

Additional elements of marketing concerns are a *business philosophy* and the *organizational structure* that includes the assignment and responsibilities for specific marketing functions. As simple as it seems, the establishment of a type of business—the nature of what is to be produced—can be a critical decision. A philosophy that inhibits change or growth can have a stultifying effect, and sometimes result in business failure. On the other hand, flexibility can contribute to sales, profit, growth and longevity.

After all, street cars rode to their own demise, railroads without outside interests are in bankruptcy, and skirt makers that did not broaden their product offerings are out of business. On the other hand, the wider definition of the nature of a business allows a firm to broaden its product base and expand its potential. As an example, Exxon's business is energy (not only oil); IBM is concerned with business information, and Phillip Morris produces cigarettes, beer and carbonated drinks.

The average or small-sized apparel producer might respond to the premises outlined by saying, "We do not have the personnel or expertise required for marketing management. It is big business oriented." Factually, big business did adopt marketing first, but it is also true that smaller-sized operators frequently use the same techniques in a more informal way. The pitfalls are that without decentralization of responsibilities and a structured system, there is often the lack of required problem concentration and a pattern of fast decision-making that lacks studied information support.

From the outset, a limited size organization should be infused with a totally planned operation that creates a favorable marketing climate for all concerned. Corporate goals should be spelled out so that there is common understanding and acceptance. It is part of management's concern to maintain some internal education program, formal or informal, that effects clear communication between management and personnel. As part of the educational process, there should be definition and assessment of marketing responsibilities, with the underlying philosophy that all efforts are to be directed toward the benefit of both the company and the consumer.

## Putting Marketing to Work

Up to this point, the discussion has been focused on theory, principles and general applications. It is now time to get closer to home and discuss more specific marketing considerations and how they can be implemented by apparel producers.

The basic premise is that every decision should be supported by data—properly researched information. Corporate goals such as organizational size, volume potential, profit potential, brand identification and market potential must be established on the basis of supportive evidence. Hunches, desire, hearsay cannot be submitted as evidence. Trade journals, management professionals and industrial and government figures are among other sources that are easily available.

Marketing objectives should be selected carefully, and in line with corporate goals. For example, if they are vague—to sell 5,000 price maintaining stores, use of a travelling road staff, to produce four lines a year, to produce merchandise for reorders—they are meaningless unless the product is sufficiently unique to attract and impress store buyers.

Buyers are professionals who weigh the relative importance of market offerings and finally select merchandise that merits stock inclusion. A buyer's purchases are restrained by a merchandise plan which confines commitments to merchandise which has estimated salability and profit-making potential. In a market of abundance, the producer must be sufficiently objective to say to himself: "Why should a seasoned buyer purchase my goods?" And just as important, when a buyer's answer is negative, to listen. Tuning out feedback is a dangerous practice.

What to make, for what delivery, at what price and·in what quantities are nagging and constant apparel producer problems. The answers to these "whats" must be sufficiently satisfactory to customers for the business to stay alive—much more so for it to be highly successful. Fashion is a unique product in an opportunistic market, and the apparel producer's task is to produce a line or collection that is the result of a thoroughly thought out study.

Is it new and exciting enough to pre-empt what customers own presently? Is it in line with current lifestyle? Is it competitive? Is it promotable (newsworthy)?

And most important, perhaps, will the purchase of the produced line cause a state of betterment for both retailers and consumers? For the former, betterment is an anticipated or better rate of sale; for the latter, the satisfaction of one or a combination of emotional motivations. Rational consumer purchase motivations play a part in the purchase decision, but for apparel they are a minor influence.

## Consumer Behavior

Areas of research for style development should include textile companies, retailers and people. A top notch apparel producer must wear the hat of an amateur psychologist—one who has a working knowledge of consumer behavior, particularly as it affects the purchase of fashion apparel. Psychographics is one of the newest social sciences that is now incorporated into the study of consumer behavior as part of marketing. Therefore, as a principle and a practice, a line must be the result of researched information, the major sources of information being: suppliers, channels of distribution, designers and executive judgment.

Marketing strategies—sales force size, selling techniques, channels of distribution, pricing and sales promotion activities—should be interlocking functions, each with standards of performance and reviews of achievement. Feedback and marketing intelligence should be an integral part of the marketing process. Information should be solicited from disparate evidence—customers, vendors, salespeople, records, etc. The information should be collected, analyzed and used to determine what to add, delete or change in the current and future lines.

In the fashion industry, marketing is an integrated system for most textile concerns, particularly for those of large size. During the past 10 years, there has been hardly an issue of a trade publication that has not featured marketing as a vital subject. More recently, retailers have made a distinction, and now are practicing both merchandising and marketing. In fact, the following quotation from a major New York daily newspaper sums up current thinking succinctly:

"Retail executives, long accustomed to thinking of themselves as day-to-day purveyors of goods, now—by force of circumstances—

find themselves being referred to in rounded terms as 'retail marketers.'"

It should be apparent that it is insufficient for an apparel producer to employ marketing on a haphazard basis. Marketing is more than a procedure or staffing function. The ingredients include:

- A philosophy;
- A system;
- Goals and objectives;
- Research;
- Strategies and tactics;
- Evaluation.

Survival in apparel manufacturing in the future will lean heavily on marketing expertise.

## 2. PLANNING A MARKETING PROGRAM: WHERE TO BEGIN

The most basic elements of marketing are getting the right goods to the right people at the right prices by using the right promotional means. The goal of all marketing efforts—profit—is overwhelmingly the result of affirmative responses to these "rights." But the required critical analysis to achieve them is often frustrating; and when decisions are conceived improperly they can lead to business dislocation, the extreme of which is bankruptcy.

Modern business is characterized by widely-known technology, easily obtained; events that are broadcast instantaneously, and product sameness. *Product exclusivity is a rarity,* and even if owned, only a temporary marketing advantage. But producers are charged with the onus to develop products that are "different"—more consumer-satisfying, having at least some components that add up to a more customer-pleasing arrangement. The profusion of T.V. commercials that feature *non sequitur* themes, hardly related to product quality or genuine serviceability, bear testament to this widespread similarity.

All marketers are concerned with the assessment of market opportunity, a potential customer group, and strength of competing firms. These are essential initial marketing undertakings. The steps that follow are the concerns and research required to develop products with sufficient desirability to attain a calculated market share.

Creating the right fashion apparel is a weighty problem in a market that has more producers than are needed. The market fit of products in the fashion business is dependent upon customer demand that is constantly shifting, and survival is dependent upon maintaining pace with that demand.

There are no rules, adages, or principles that guarantee success, but there are considerations that should be studied to enhance the possibilities of fulfilling the marketing "rights," and avoid the cardinal sin of fashion marketing—"being out of trend."

The constant "article of faith" should be the very definition of fashion—*that which is accepted by a substantial group of people at a given time and place.* If this definition is fully conceptualized and products are developed accordingly, there will be a constant endeavor to cater to the whims and dictates of the final arbiter, the supreme judge who decides what and when styles become fashion: the consumer.

It can be said with certainty that apparel marketing involves a unique product in a unique environment. Successful firms are aware that the built-in values and/or conditions—low intrinsic value relationship, seasonality, constant change, high emotion, and the need for high levels of stock turnover and markdowns—all add up to producer vulnerability.

## Consumer Loyalty

Consumer loyalty is the *quid pro quo* of fashion currency. And fashion marketing difficulty is further exacerbated by an atmosphere in which it is relatively easy to start a new business, since capital requirement is less than practically any other manufacturing business, and by the means in which most apparel is developed—"knocking off" or mutating the styles of others. Is it any wonder that the number of manufacturers are predicted to be reduced by one-third by the year 1985 (helped in no small degree by foreign competition)?

A major premise is that an apparel producer should recognize and base all product decisions on the repeated pattern of consumer fashion acceptance, and how it is finally sold. These factors are exemplified by the diagram in Figure 1.

The key issue is the careful selection of a customer group(s). If this decision is on target, the type of styling, price levels, channels of distribution, promotional strategies, and other important marketing activities can be developed most appropriately. It follows, therefore, that the selection of the innovative group (willing and able to pay highest prices) is the concentration on the most limited audience (2½ percent), one that seeks prophetic styling. And on the other hand, the middle groups of early and late majorities comprise the bulk of the market, but in an arena of greatest competition, including entrenched resources, some of which are branded and "married" to stores. Hence, the fundamental question is: "Where are my customers and how can I satisfy them?"

The targeting of a customer group must include the consideration that purchase behavior is motivated by the consumer's desire to seek a state of betterment. In this search, the consumer exercises

*Strategies and Tactics in Fashion Marketing*

FIGURE 1

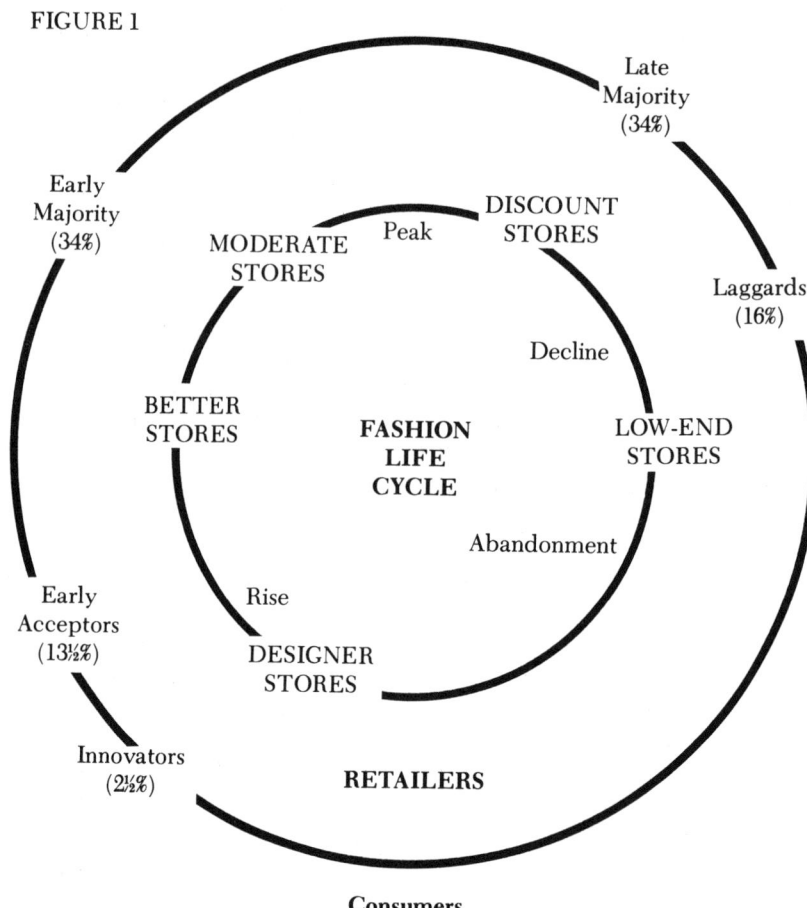

the option of creating apparel obsolescence, "the rejection of present ownership in favor of newness, even though the old still retains utility value." With this in mind, styling must include sufficient newness to age what consumers own. But "how new" is the rub. "Too new" will not be accepted by most. The acceptance of newness, most often, requires sophistication and wherewithal.

It is safe to say that the better price customer wants complete newness, high fashion (accepted by a few); the moderate price group wants what it can comprehend and is in trend; and the popular price customer sector, for the most part, wants the combination of trend and price appeal. A manufacturer, therefore, can select a potential customer group and develop merchandise on the basis of:

- Market size (numbers)
- Timing of customer purchases

- Appropriate price level

## "Late Is Cheap"

The last of the above, pricing, is the linchpin of marketing strategy. A market truism, "to be later is to be cheaper," holds except in periods of temporary shortages. The dilemma is that once prices are set, based on all cost factors and profit, any downward revision upsets retail customers (except late or out of season) and reduces planned profit, not to speak of loss of prestige.

The apparel producer does not enjoy the advantage of producers of many other products, the option of selecting one of two major pricing policies: "skimming the cream" or "penetration price strategy." Following the former, prices are deliberately set high to attain an initial high markup, with the plan to lower prices later; in the latter strategy, prices are set for immediate market penetration and to discourage competition.

Penetration price strategy may be a way of life for the few who by reason of manufacturing advantage can "knock-off" popular styles to do volume business. Working on short markup, however, may be a dangerous way to live. Prices should be carefully planned on the basis of objectives, some of which are:

- End-user appeal requirement.
- The ability to attain sufficient revenue and profit.
- The product's ability to escape direct and immediate competition.
- Appeal requirement for retail stores that are proper channels of distribution for intended ultimate consumers.

Product strategy should include the aim of maintaining continued ultimate and retail customer support—the only sure way to organization longevity. A manufacturer who owns a well-identified brand is in a most fortuitous position, since a true brand assumes consumer product identification and ability to buy it with relative ease. A brand, therefore, includes the condition of wide retail distribution.

In a highly competitive environment, the average manufacturer does not have the required combination of financing and expertise to generate this market position. Every effort, therefore, should be made to concentrate on products that have sufficient characteristics to deserve continued retail stocking—day-to-day selling styles. This takes forebearance, the avoidance of fads and other short-lived items. This tack entails the utilization of strong efforts to establish strong store relationships—i.e., the selling of groups of styles with thematic approaches that are in trend. Additionally, the relationship, particularly with important retailers, should include the exchange of ideas for mutual benefit.

Successful manufacturers research trends and build a variety of styles around those selected for line inclusion. But, regardless of intra-organizational strength—a talented designer, respected executive judgment, or a proven record of "know how"—a line's research effort should include input from retail store buyers. And finally, when a line is complete, there should be a consensus of important retail customer intentions, a strong indicator of probable line strength.

In the final analysis, a manufacturer's strength is founded on his contribution to retailer profit, which is the result of consumer acceptance. In order to reach the highest level of retail store resource, an apparel firm must contribute to departmental character and the aforementioned profit.

In summary, some of the major considerations in planning an apparel line should be:

- Fashion is an end result of consumer acceptance.
- Merchandise must be important to certain customers and certain retailers.
- Styling must cause obsolescence.
- Pricing should be related to the selected customer group, competition, product market strength, and the producer's reputation.
- Universal insecurity of consumer decisions demands input by outside respected professionals.
- Objective evaluation should be carried out after line completion.

## 3. PLANNING A RETAIL DISTRIBUTION SYSTEM

A widespread and balanced roster of retail store customers, distribution in all major regions and in effective numbers in given trading areas, is the goal of all manufacturers. But these attainments are highly elusive and enjoyed by few.

Probably more marketing effort is extended to establish and maintain a distribution system than any other marketing activity. This effort is well-placed because an effective system is the very heart of manufacturing success. Distribution system and channel of distribution are synonymous terms, the conduit by which products flow from producer to ultimate consumer.

A distribution system, by necessity, is a mutual relationship between producer and retailer, both of whom have similar purposes —to obtain profit by supplying consumers with products they want, when they want them, at the prices they will pay for them, and in quantities they can absorb. These terms, except profit, add up to

## Fashion Marketing Concepts

what is commonly referred to as "consumer orientation"—the recognition of customer desires.

Since annual retail sales in the U.S. are approaching the "sound barrier" of one trillion dollars—a figure that could be reached in 1980 or shortly after—it is apparent that we have an effective national retail system. There is hardly a shortage of stores. But the manufacturer's task is to establish profitable relations with the *right* stores, with sufficient uniformity of characteristics for maximum appeal to intended consumers.

The apparel business, with a current annual retail volume in the neighborhood of $85 billion, has available some 170,000 stores that have a significant interest in fashion merchandise. In an intensively competitive environment in which there is a surplus of apparel manufacturers, the ability to distribute goods to proper outlets and maintain a level of retail importance is a most difficult task.

The difficulty starts with the need for a product that pre-empts other manufacturers, or having merchandise that deserves store inclusion by reason of some unique quality that is recognized first by store buyers and later by end-users. In this environment, if "uniqueness" fades and the selling rate slows down, a manufacturer is bypassed by a competitor. Loyalty to resources is not a retailer attribute, and rightly so in a business that is opportunistic.

The ability to choose a distribution system, therefore, is predicated on a manufacturer's "know-how," some manufacturing advantage and/or products that are worthy of retailer acceptance and probably consumer-satisfying.

The most basic consideration is: "Who are my retailers?" This fundamental query is based on the need to distribute goods to outlets that have some uniformity of goals, the most compelling of which is a prime position with the manufacturer's intended consumer group. Different types of retailers have characteristics that are peculiar to them, which are recognized by their customers who categorize them in order of importance for particular apparel purchases.

For example, why do men prefer specialty shops? Why do mass distributors own a better share of children's apparel than adult clothing? Why is cruise apparel purchased at better priced stores? What type of customer buys apparel in discount stores? Essentially, the answers relate to consumer orientation, but to put them into different terms because of their importance, consumers seek the three utilities of place, ownership and time—purchasing goods at the place where they want them when they are wanted. In response to these demands, every retailer establishes a mix of store location, merchandising policies (assortment, depth, price levels, etc.), services and communication. These strategies are designed to best serve a segmented group and influence its patronage.

*Strategies and Tactics in Fashion Marketing*

The choice of retailer type, therefore, hinges on merchandise strength: its importance to particular types of ultimate customers, the degree of effort they will exert to acquire it, and where they will shop for it. Specialty goods—those that appeal to a specialized customer group—must have specific characteristics for which the customers will expend a special effort to acquire them. On the other hand, impulse and convenience goods will impel little or no effort. Most apparel falls into a fourth group, shopping goods, the kind that are purchased only after customer comparison of offerings of more than one store.

These consumer behavior patterns lead to the need to select one of three distribution systems: 1) franchise, 2) selective, or 3) open (intensive).

The *franchise* system extends prescribed exclusivity to stores, and is generally used by those who produce "exclusive" merchandise —high priced designer-name styles. Since better-priced customers seek merchandise of limited distribution, they are willing to travel to purchase them and have the rigidity not to accept substitutes. The manufacturer's advantage of taking this tack are: the assurance of appropriate customers, retail and consumer; strongest retailer loyalty, and a low level of retail competition.

The *selective* system is the most widely used. The vast majority of makers cater to early and late majority customers, and depend upon road sales personnel to judiciously place goods in the proper number of stores so that competition is at a reasonable level, and insuring a balance between stores and population. An organization with a well-developed marketing system breaks the country into trading areas and targets a specific number of stores in each one, often including particular stores of major trading area importance. For example, in Chicago, Marshall Field or Carson Pirie Scott and certain specialty stores that do a yearly volume of at least $500,000 might be targeted.

The *open (intensive)* system is suited best for popular priced merchandise in a highly competitive market, and often is reflective of low manufacturer markup. Using this strategy, any retail organization that merits credit facilities is a potential customer.

Success is not infrequently based on a wise selection of a proper distribution system, although there is frequent need to use alternate methods in the face of competition. Therefore, a marketer's conclusions must be founded on his product's relationship to consumer buying habits, the need for certain type(s) of retailers, and having the ability to apply the appropriate strategy to influence these retailers.

There are additional aspects that should be considered to avoid later problems. Large specialty and department stores decentralize their departments by prices, sizes, lifestyle, etc., which are designed to enhance consumer patronage motives. It is therefore necessary to study each store's departmental set-up and try to obtain uniform distribution.

As a case in point, a number of years ago, a well-known sweater manufacturer, at the point of first establishing his distribution, was successful in making an arrangement with a resident buying office representative for the distribution of his line to member stores. Since the stores were nationally known institutions, the manufacturer was elated.

But the arrangement was a mistake of hugh proportion. Why? The resident representative serviced junior sized sportswear departments in which the styling had limited appeal. After ten years, despite considerable effort, he was successful in changing only five of 25 departments. His volume was about one-third of what it could have been. As a practical measure, if initial efforts to sell the right department are not successful, it may be well not to settle for second best; there is always another day and another opportunity. As a matter of fact, transference of department, even with buyer approval, in some stores, requires that a resource must remain fallow for one year before another department can use the manufacturer.

As part of distribution strategies, manufacturers often use such inducements as a selling force, such as co-operative advertising, markdown money, the return of poor sellers, and other store-advantage selling terms. What and how much is extended depends upon the manufacturer's reputation, market position and competition. A manufacturer with a healthy business offers least, sometimes nothing; one with weakness most. There are no rules to guide what must be given; the circumstances of need and what can be gained are, probably, the best responses.

Most manufacturers aim for a national distribution. The consideration to achieve this status is: "Does the line have importance to all sections of the country in sizing, color, weight, fabric, detail and silhouette?" The line, of necessity, must be analyzed as to its importance in each region, and additional elements included if necessary.

Indeed, the planning of a retail distribution system and maintaining it requires deep and constant concentration. It is the hub of marketing activities because it leads to planned volume, which in turn is the reason for the wheels of production to turn, and the condition of profit making. A distribution system should be the end result of a calculated plan and effort.

## 4. SELLING—A MARKETING ACTIVITY

### Introduction

The reason for being in business is to make a profit by exchanging a product or service at a price that includes ample markup (profit). It is for good reason that a profit and loss statement starts with sales, followed by deductions for cost of goods and/or services and expenses, and ends with a profit or loss figure, usually referred to as the bottom line.

When a firm's products or services are in strong demand, it is in the best position to command a price that assures profit. But when competition is intense and the market has product abundance and sameness, selling conditions must be created so that buyers perceive the offerings as valuable. In other terms, successful selling in a competitive environment hinges on the ability to pre-empt the products and efforts of others.

In a society of abundance, there are few, if any, "mousetraps" that cause customers to beat paths to producers' doors. The onus is on sellers to offer consumers what they want—when—and at prices consistent with consumer equation of value. Even in rare instances of shortages, options are still available to consumers. For example, if sugar reaches an abnormally high price, consumers can exercise cross-elasticity—the selection of a substitute product at a lesser cost that serves the same purpose, like honey or an artificial sweetener. Hence, our business environment is characterized by a constant race among competitors to attract customer patronage by communicating the value of what they are selling.

In response to widespread product availability and technological know-how, business firms formalized their activities to have the best chances to attain organizational goals, to respond to marketing opportunities, to make the most effective assignment of responsibilities to personnel, and finally, to attain maximum planned sales and profit. Over the years, with greatest concentration during the period 1950 to 1970, these activities became more sophisticated with the development of computer-based information systems and trained specialists. Modern marketing became a fact of business life.

### Definition of Marketing

Marketing has almost as many definitions as there are practitioners. Most professionals are prone to describe marketing in terms of their own responsibilities. Although experts rarely agree on the definition, they do concur on the activities of marketing (discussed later in this chapter). The American Marketing Association on *Defi-*

*nitions* says that marketing is "the performance of business activities that direct the flow of goods and services from producer to consumer or user." Paul Mazur, a nationally respected marketer, said years ago, "Marketing is the delivery of a standard of living to society." Professor McNair of Harvard added a concept to this definition by adding one word so that it reads, "Marketing is the creation and delivery of a standard of living to society."

These definitions relate to broad concepts and for our purpose do not offer sufficient details "to hang our hats on." Therefore, for our discussion, "Marketing is a total business interaction that includes the planning, pricing, promotion, and distribution of consumer-wanted goods and/or services for a corporate profit."

This definition highlights a subject that is pertinent to our discussion—the importance of the role the consumer plays in the selling process, the selecter of wanted goods and/or services. By analyzing the definition more closely, the following implications are also apparent:

1. Total business interaction implies a system in which activities are structured and assigned to team members.
2. Planning is the foundation of decisions.
3. Pricing recognizes the importance of establishing a balance between cost and value.
4. Promotion concedes the need to communicate effectively with consumers.
5. Consumer-wanted products is admission that the consumer is the decision-maker of product or service value.
6. Distribution implies that successful selling depends upon the selection of proper channels that have open lives to appropriate consumers.
7. Profit is the end-result of marketing efficiency.

## Historical Development of Marketing

Every commercial organization is a marketing structure that functions for the purposes of creating profit through selling.

Early in history, selling effort was of minor significance because most people were engaged largely in producing for self-consumption. However, when production eventually exceeded the ability to consume one's own output, there was need to seek buyers to absorb product overages. At first, efforts were minimal since customers could be found locally. As production grew and exceeded the capacity of local consumption, selling became more complex with the need to seek distant markets. And in due course, even foreign trading areas reached a stage of saturation for some products and forced producers to develop strategies to outflank other sellers by applying more sophisticated marketing techniques.

In the United States, the first marketing concentration was based on an agrarian or backwoods economy. The vast majority of Americans were concerned with agriculture and were more or less self-sufficient. Selling to a great degree was conducted as a barter system.

During the mid-nineteenth century, the Industrial Revolution reached our shores from England. With our entry into the Industrial Age, concentration was focused on mass production. Products started to roll off assembly lines, but there was no difficulty in selling them in a market of sufficient consumers with money and willingness to buy mass-produced goods.

Around 1920, approximately 75 years after the inception of mass production, some products began to exceed demand, the condition of a "buyer's market" (when supply exceeds demand). It became necessary to give more consideration to consumers in the form of newer styles, cheaper prices, and other consumer-satisfying elements to maintain an equilibrium between productive capacity and the ability to sell. Selling became a more concentrated business focal point, and the term marketing became more common to the business vocabulary.

During World War II industries expanded with concentration on war material. Civilian shortages became a way of life. After the conflict, pent-up demand for products were easily satisfied as a consequence of widened production facilities and the application of new technology. Competition for consumer patronage became more heated. The importance of marketing grew with producers' realization that products are only successful where they respond to consumer wants.

In the decade of 1960–1970, competition was further intensified in many markets due to an unprecedented flow of products from foreign markets. Producers were given the mandate to intensify their efforts on planning, producing, and distributing merchandise that consumers are likely to want—when—where—at what prices—and in what quantitites. The period became known as the era of consumer orientation—the time when marketing took into full account consumer conditions for product (or service) acceptance.

During the following decade, 1970–1980, marketing entered another period—the era of the total marketing concept. New consumer characteristics, increased use of technology, and unrelenting domestic and foreign competition caused the realization that to succeed an organization must establish a chain of strong links. Accordingly, the marketing thrust of enlightened organizations assigned particular activities and responsibilities to trained personnel and pro-

# Fashion Marketing Concepts

vided intra-organizational communication channels to integrate all marketing activities. This meshing process is actually a system by which problems and opportunities are identified, studied, and analyzed by people working in concert to maximize the possibility of attaining organizational goals.

## Marketing Activities

In our economy there are two basic processes: one is production —the creation of goods and services; the other is marketing—the activities by which goods and services flow from producer to ultimate consumer.

It should be noted that production is not a marketing activity, but product planning, scheduling, servicing and physical distribution and warehousing are included in the range of marketing activities.

The manner in which merchandising activities are performed vary with type of business. As examples, the main activities of retailing are buying at wholesale and selling in retail quantities and prices. A manufacturer, on the other hand, plans and produces products. Therefore, product planning and development relate to different practices, depending upon the business sector. Standardizing and grading are concerned with either goods purchased or produced. Buying and selling can refer to finished goods for resale or materials required for additional processes before resale. Selling is a marketing constant for all firms, the only means by which profit is attained.

## The Marketing System

A marketing system is structured so that selected strategies and tactics can be planned, implemented, and adjusted to an ever-changing environment. Marketing, therefore, requires a sensitivity to trends—the direction in which the environment is headed—and relative rapid adjustment of strategies and tactics to accommodate them.

A market environment has two sets of conditions or influences, uncontrollable and controllable. A system's successful operation must be constructed in a manner that responds effectively to the pressures of both.

Figure 1 illustrates:

1. The target of marketing activities—consumers,
2. The marketing system—controllable factors, and
3. The external or uncontrollable factors.

## Uncontrollable (External) Factors

The efficiency of a marketing system is measured by the speed with which decisions respond to environmental change, the accuracy

FIGURE 1

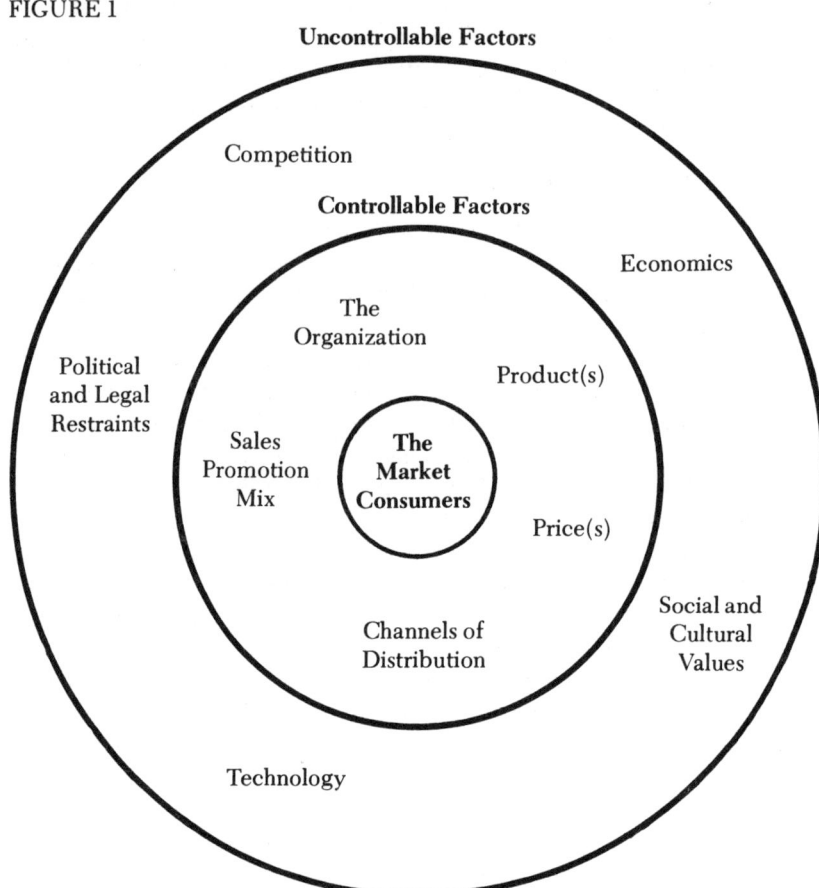

of forecasting the direction and intensity of change, and the selection of the most appropriate action to accommodate change.

Marketing executives are conversant with the broad aspects of the external environment. There is universal knowledge of the existence of competition, and the realization of what does not exist today will probably develop tomorrow, particularly when there is established business success. The level of expected competition is proportionate to the opportunity for profit. The exceptions are sectors that are monopolies created by government or virtual cartels that are able to discourage competition by their size and entrenched position, such as the automobile business.

A firm's ability to sell its products is most often related to economic conditions. The elements of a viable market are represented by sufficient potential customers with a willingness and ability to buy.

Fundamental conditions of selling are that products must be technologically feasible and producible at prices that consumers are willing to pay. Automobiles, for example, that operate on one gallon of gasoline for 100 miles would find a vast market. The inhibiting factor is that such a car is not within the range of production capability.

Social and cultural values are strong influences in dictating purchase behavior. These factors are major forces in setting product suitability for customer groups. As a well-known example, could blue jeans have become the most important international fashion in the 1940's or 1950's? It took a confluence of events in the 1960's to create a social and cultural atmosphere that fostered the acceptance of this most casual fashion.

Political and legal restraints are marketing guidelines established by local, state, and federal governments within which business firms must operate. Anti-trust laws, pricing legislation, and regulatory measures affect advertising, packaging, selling terms, distribution systems, and the products themselves. Political and legal forces exercise more influence or marketing activities than any other major area of business operation.

## Controllable Factors

A firm operates its marketing system with regard for the influences and constraints of the external environment, with the purposes of reaching a selected market group and satisfying it in a manner that is profitable to the operation. In order to reach these goals, a set of controllable factors are developed:

- The organization
- The product(s)
- The price(s)
- Channels of distribution
- Sales promotion mix.

These ingredients are blended, and modified when there is failure or inadequate consumer response and/or profitability.

The product is the prime ingredient of an organization's existence, the means by which sales are generated. In the development of a product or line there is consideration of what makes for consumer-satisfying qualities or expectations, such as: brand name importance, color assortment, and packaging.

Price level is related to profit, sometimes a competitive "weapon," and evidence of a product's value as compared to similar market offerings. Its influence in motivating consumer purchase behavior is considerable.

Channels of distribution are the conduits by which products flow and eventually reach ultimate consumers. The policy of required characteristics of channels of distribution are established by management after careful diliberation, since distribution success is based on the producer's goal to reach the right consumers. In this mutual relationship, it is sales personnel who act as communicators to effect the transference of title in the product flow from the initial production stage to the time it is placed in the hands of the end-user.

Sales promotion involves all activities of communication directed to consumers, among which are: advertising, public relations, display, and personal selling; all designed to influence potential consumers to favor an advertiser's product or service.

One of the most common and effective marketing strategies is the use of a sales force which engages in the personal activity of sales promotion. When a company develops a line of merchandise, requires selling, changes its product, or simply wants to increase sales, the most productive and responsive means is personal selling. Personal selling is a costly activity, but it is highly productive and the core of most firms' sales promotion strategy.

Controllable factors are often referred to as the marketing mix—a matrix of planned elements designed to develop:

- Competitive products
- Customer patronage—initial and continued
- Planned distribution
- Profit.

Other marketing goals could include the establishment of a brand name or the attainment of a planned percentage of a particular market.

## The Marketing Structure

In order to establish an effective relationship between producer and consumer, marketing activities are arranged so that there is a logical flow of communication and delivery of consumer-accepted products. Figure 2 exemplifies how marketing activities are planned and practiced to attain corporate goals, also known as the marketing process.

For a business to realize the full value of a marketing system, there should be a chart of organization that assigns responsibilities and performance of specified functions. Figure 3 is a chart of organization that shows how marketing activities can be integrated and applied to the marketing process.

## Summary

Each day we use innumerable goods and services—to eat, to wear, to protect us from the elements and to decorate our bodies, or

*Fashion Marketing Concepts*

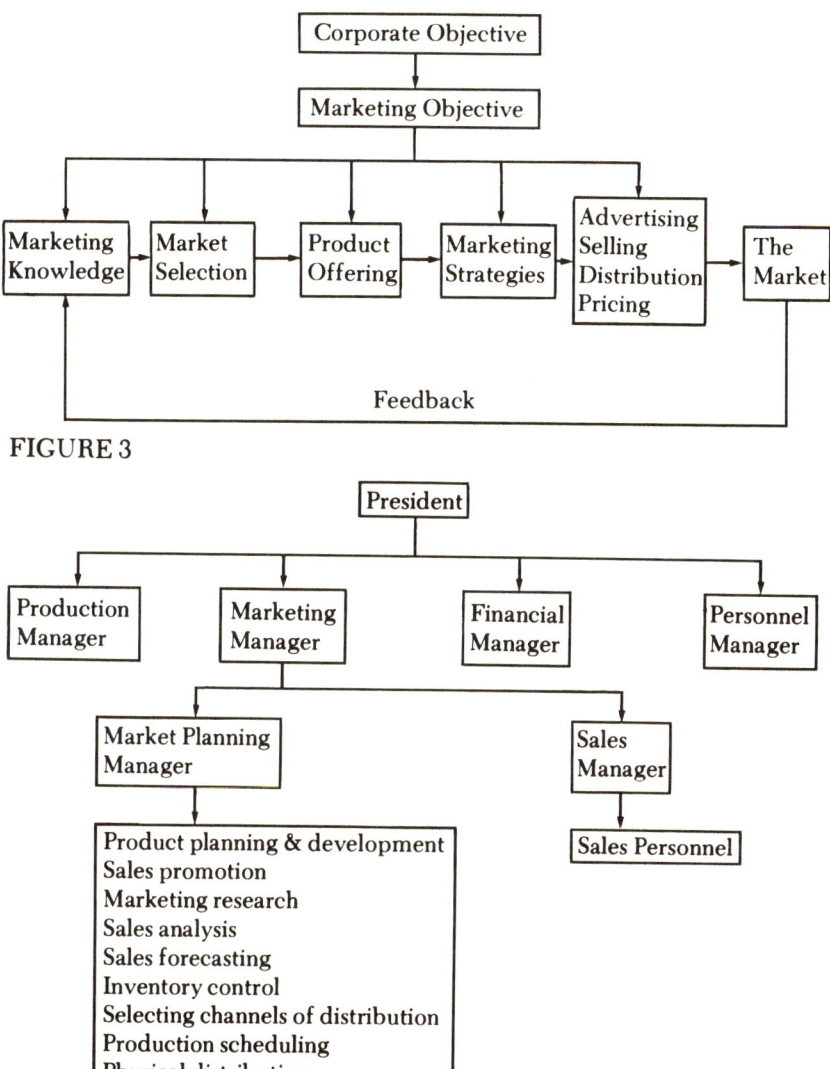

FIGURE 2

FIGURE 3

simply to enjoy. We give little thought to how many people played a part in providing these goods and services.

It is natural to assume that some orderly process took place to ensure the planning, production, and distribution of the "right" products, at the "right" prices, available in the "right" places, and in the "right" quantities.

In a capitalistic system, competition is fostered. When there is opportunity for profit, there is considerable or intense competition.

When our country was young, there was no need for a business to have an organized system to sell goods. However, as the nation matured and developed technology to produce goods in greater quantities for vastly increased numbers of people, and business activity more than kept pace with these developments, competition became intense. Similar products became profuse. More often than not, merchandise difference became more cosmetic than real.

In this environment selling became increasingly difficult, profit had to be planned through a system, a set of arranged activities so related and connected as to form a unity of purpose—the attainment of corporate goals—the most important of which is to sell goods or service to realize profit. The categories of activities evolved into merchandising, physical distribution, and supporting activities, which became the umbrella of organizational functions—modern marketing.

Selling is the fundamental purpose of every business. Therefore, sales personnel are employed to contact potential customers, to educate them, and to prove a product's answer to a need. The main objective of salespeople is to present the foregoing and to culminate a transaction whereby there is a transference of goods or services to serve consumer needs. Sales people are the "field soldiers" of a business organization, integral, prime performers of a marketing team.

To be effective, selling requires the cooperation of all personnel of an organization. With the continuing trend to larger and more complicated business structures and more complex products, it is increasingly important for all departments of an organization's marketing team to work together to provide customers with the best products at prices that reflect higher value than the cost.

When a marketing system functions properly, salespeople are highly regarded communicators. They are able to keep management informed of competition, customer requests, market trends, and new product opportunities.

A salesperson's basic role in the marketing process is:

- to sell,
- to inform, and
- to follow through on sales.

An organization's main concern is to make a profit through selling the function of salespeople—key cogs of a well-functioning marketing system.

# SECTION TWO

# Planning

As NOTED IN the introduction of Section One, the common approach to all marketing activities is *planning*. Although each fashion business sector operates at a different level in the flow of the product, from the production of its material to the final stage of placing it in the hands of the ultimate consumer, each has its focus on the consumer market (end-users).

Each sector has different time frames for planning. The textile industry requires up to years to develop a product. Some manufacturers require minimal lead time, they "knock-off" styles; while others that develop more or less original styling must plan up to a year in advance of a seasonal line completion. Retailers' plans fall into two categories: short range, a six-month plan performed by a member of the merchandising staff; and the long-range, developed by management.

The generic "problems" of fashion marketing include:
- What to produce (or buy)?
- When?
- At what price?
- In what quantity?
- Where will it sell best?
- Why?

The articles in this section address themselves to some aspects of these questions from the vantage points of the different levels of the industry:

>Articles 5 and 6—apparel producers and retailers.
>Article 7—apparel producers.
>Article 8—textile sector, apparel producers, retailers.
>Article 9—textile sector, apparel producers, retailers.
>Article 10—small store entrepreneurs.

## 5. HOW TO ASSESS CONSUMER BUYING POWER

Apparel producers and retailers are monitoring current economic conditions and their influence on consumer buying behavior.

Obviously, the future outlook does not include the conditions of a viable fashion market environment—people with money and a willingness to spend it. The average consumer is beset by the effects of a recurring recession, relentless inflation, and escalating oil and energy costs. In face of these pressures, consumers are re-evaluating their assortment of needs and categorizing some as questionable luxuries. Simply put, people, of necessity, are changing their purchase priorities, and establishing new lifestyles which affect their apparel purchase attitudes.

From a marketer's point of view, a vigil must be maintained to discern consumer changes of attitudes about:

- style importance
- prices
- purchase frequency
- where, when, and how to purchase

Successful marketing will depend upon early recognition of changes and the implementation of appropriate strategies to accommodate them.

If one is looking for an optimistic note, consumers have traditionally spent approximately 8 percent of disposable income on clothing. As a case in point, the Department of Labor's Bureau of Labor statistics estimated that a hypothetical urban family of four needed $18,622 to live comfortably in 1978. This gross income equates as a disposable income of $14,953 ($18,622 less income tax and social security) of which $1,209 was spent on clothing—8 percent plus.

In 1979, it was estimated that the median family income had risen to $17,600. But the downside is that a vast number of families were forced to spend up to 90 percent of their disposable income on the necessities of food, housing, energy, transportation, and medical care. Although the dollar figure of disposable income will probably remain at 8 percent, there will be changes in consumer attitude about clothing purchase priorities—undoubtedly a more qualitative selection of options within the aforementioned areas.

Marketing approaches to new consumer attitudes by producers and retailers will vary from firm to firm. Unanimity, however, will be the realization that unsold inventory is the sure road to organizational dislocation, and some degree of production or purchase caution will have to be exercised. The response to selling uncertainty has always been a controlled inventory level, a practice that supports the following theory: When business is booming a retailer will stock merchandise like a jobber; when business is "normal" the apparel manufacturer will carry inventory; when business is "fair" the textile producer will maintain inventory; and when business is poor no one carries inventory.

## A V-P's Point of View

The marketing vice-president of a giant-size women's manufacturer, part of a conglomerate, offered his company's marketing philosophy in response to the current environment, which may be the strategy of many large-scale producers:

> "We do about $80 million a year, which necessitates a distribution to thousands of stores, many of whom influence other retailers in their trading areas. Our merchandise targets the upper-lower and lower-middle income groups of ultimate consumers. In the light of current conditions, our styling must be safe, middle-of-the-road merchandise. In other words, as we see it, consumers have become more rational in their purchasing and select styles that have the longest fashion life.
>
> "Stores see our merchandise as the backbone of their stock composition, and therefore can buy in depth for both day-to-day selling and in preparation for promotional events. It is our opinion, based on current success, that this method of marketing eliminates the contingency of high markdowns and offers the ultimate consumer the best value.
>
> "If one compares the value of today's merchandise, a dumb blouse at $27 retail is no bargain—not by far. But, on the other hand, this item has wardrobe flexibility, it can match or coordinate with other items in our groupings, or be used with the consumer's wardrobe components. Frankly, this is a depression-proof strategy. Customer newness can be attained with the purchase of one component of an outfit.
>
> "As part of our strategy, we have built an "escape hatch" into our method of merchandising. We produce four times a year, but do not produce merchandise for reorders. Once we collect and collate a season's orders, we produce, ship, and then start to work on the next season. It is the retailer's responsibility to order a sufficient amount of goods to cover an entire season's need.
>
> "Prices reflect current costs: what costs more is priced higher. We are not locked into price levels."

This approach includes the elements of safety. The elimination of reorders is not an innovative marketing ploy. Better priced houses have always followed the practice of selling, cutting to orders, delivering, and ending a season with no reorders, except for some special orders. Some multi-unit retail organizations, in fact, currently prefer the "in and out" approach to merchandising moderate priced lines. Using this method, retail stocks can have initial stock depth, in-house promotional quantities, and enjoy some of the advantages of doing business with big firms as key resources.

The advantages of large scale purchasing from giants include

*Strategies and Tactics in Fashion Marketing*

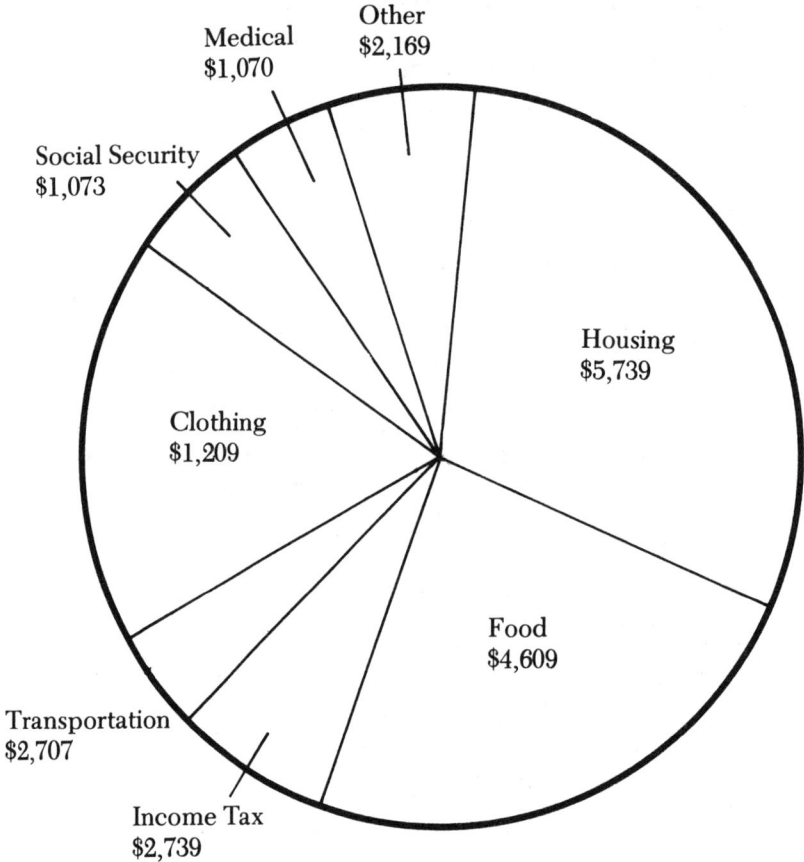

the "unmentionables" of assured liberal cooperative advertising and markdown money, store-advantage terms that are of no small significance when business is "tough." Another factor is that widespread foreign purchases have taught stores how to operate with one delivery for an entire season.

The vice-president of a nationally known department store organization offered his views:

> "We learned a lesson in 1979. Shoe prices, for example, went sky-high, and we followed the quality upward to new established retail levels, basically from $75 to $100. These new price points had a fair response, but our established price levels suffered because an out-of-proportion share of the open-to-buy was used for the new upper levels of our price range. We lost a considerable amount of volume by starving the heart of our operation—customer accepted price points.

*Planning*

"Our approach for 1980 takes into consideration that consumer price resistance is a vital fact of life and, if necessary, we will sacrifice quality to maintain stock strength at the traditional price levels of our departments.

"A few years ago one could make a horrendous mistake by not following quality to higher prices. Consumers were making more money and were anxious to trade-up. In fact, I remember the case of one of the largest retailers in the world that decided to hold prices. One item that I can recall was a women's slipover sweater, a "hot" seller. The buyer was instructed to hold the price by taking something out of the garment. The result was a slipover minus the back zipper. Disaster is the only word that describes the selling response.

"But today is different. The consumer is different. The consumer is questioning how high is up and battling to stretch the dollar in face of its shrinking value.

"Let us remember the priority of clothing purchases: first the children, then mother, and then last, father. Some classifications of merchandise will have to 'give.'

"Price is going to be the keynote of our strategy. We are putting strength into the lower price points of our price range."

A designer had a determined view about how fashion should be merchandised:

"As a former buyer and a current fashion director, I am appalled by the fashion sameness found in so many stores. It is apparent that manufacturers and retailers are playing it safe. The theory behind this thrust is apparently motivated by the assumption that consumers seek classically styled fashion in periods of economic stress, types that can go 'everywhere' and reflect the mood of the time.

"Even if that is the case, and I do not subscribe to it, what I do not understand is why these prosaic styles are not 'romanced.' There are so few stores that are accessorizing merchandise properly and creating an ambience that is conductive to relieving merchandise monotony. Many stores do not seem to understand that consumers might be buying more infrequently, but they are concentrating their purchases on high-priced specialty items, like handbags at $100. Today's consumer wants fewer items but better quality.

"The successful trend to designer-name jeans, in my opinion, is evidence of the consumer need to 'romance' wardrobes. A designer style in any garment but jeans would be beyond the affordable level of the average consumer's pocketbook. It is my further opinion that store selling of fashion in 1980 will be above 1979's dollar volume but off in unit sales."

Recognizing that fashion merchandising is not going to be easy in 1980, here is what the designer suggests as practical techniques:

- Stores that offer personal selling should examine their training programs. There should be a return to the basic concept that sales personnel should know how to sell fashion and do suggestive selling.

- Print-outs of merchandising events (classification reports) should be available more often than once a week. Today's requirement

*Strategies and Tactics in Fashion Marketing*

is speed, the immediate identification of developing trends and taking fast steps to exploit them.
- Stocks should reflect a sufficient quantity of 'experimental' merchandise to help sell lower priced goods. At least 15 percent of a department's inventory should be invested at price levels above the *price zone* (best selling price levels).
- Wherever possible, 3 to 5 percent of merchandise stocked should be at name designer level.
- Allocate sufficient open-to-buy for "new" resources. Playing it safe by concentrating completely on key resources tends to make stock look staid and uninteresting.

The designer continues:

"The fallacy of many upper-level stores is that they could be merchandising into the strength of discounters whose method of stock investment is to concentrate on established consumer accepted styles."

## 6. CONSUMER BUYING POWER

Fashion merchandising, a well-known retailer once said, is like driving an automobile. When conditions are favorable, with a clear road, the sun shining, and the car in good condition, the driver can have limited experience. But when conditions are bad, perhaps with ice on the ground, it may take an experienced driver to overcome the hazards.

In periods of uncertainty, it is well for a fashion marketer to draw on experience, if it is pertinent, and the experiences of those with proven records of success. Fundamentally, all estimations and/or plans are based on two premises: *experience* plus *anticipation*.

Experience would dictate that periodic reviews of the basics should be conducted. In the final analysis, ball games and business activities are founded on the proper execution of fundamentals. It would, therefore, seem proper to include a discussion of some precepts of consumer behavior as they relate to the fashion industry.

One of the realities of life is that it takes money to buy anything, and those who have more of it can buy more products at higher prices and greater frequency. As prices go up, sales are inhibited because fewer people are able or want to buy products at those levels. Even when one can afford certain prices, the consumer has two alternatives.

The first is to *compare price and value.* When the price is higher than value, the result is price resistance, the refusal to buy. The other alternative is to exercise *cross-elasticity,* the substitution of a product that serves the same purpose. For example, if dress prices rise sharply, the rate of sale may diminish since the consumer can opt to purchase a skirt or a blouse to pep up her present wardrobe to make a new outfit.

*Planning*

A consumer's need for information about fashion is more critical than any other product because the very nature of fashion, as we know it, includes the element of change. Therefore, in an age when consumers have mobility and wide choice, the average consumer is likely to do more shopping and comparing of value.

The growing importance of supermarket discount coupons is evidence that consumers are bent upon making a concerted effort to obtain the most for the dollar. Shopping is a form of education, and a budget-pressed consumer will shop, compare, and make fashion buying decisions based on value potential.

A discussion that highlights the basics of consumer behavior is apt to place too much emphasis on rationalized consumer decisions to purchase apparel. By far, fashion merchandising is dependent upon psychological obsolescence, and that is a point that should never be omitted from a fashion marketer's thinking. Above all, consumers seek a state of betterment to express the four-part self-concept theory:

- This is who I am.
- This is who I would like to be.
- This is what people think of me.
- This is what I would like people to think of me.

## Motivating Consumers

The specific reasons for the purchase of apparel are too lengthy for our purpose, but current purchasing of designer name jeans must include the motivation of status and peer evaluation. Therefore, despite the apparent need to recognize the possibility of outpricing an embattled consumer, the contingency of consumers exercising cross-elasticity, and the need to market "sensibly," there is still the need for producers and retailers to entice consumers to discard present ownership in favor of the newer.

In this environment there is no shortage of merchandise and stores. Therefore, there must be evidence of what the consumer perceives as value: the suitability of the merchandise to the consumer's purpose, and product excitement. The consumer's emotional motivation can be heightened in an atmosphere that excites and permits the consumer to fantasize how new apparel can cause a state of betterment.

It is safe to predict that the sales of fashion merchandise for 1980 will maintain their proportionate share of consumers' disposable income. But the more important questions are *what will they buy, at what frequency, at what price, in what quantities, and from whom?*

Stores will select and implement marketing strategies geared to their segmented customer groups. Following is a selected range of probable courses of action:

- Unquestionably there will be a more intensified retail concentration on price promotions stressing unusual value. Shorter retail markup, producer concessions, and specification merchandise are within the range of possibilities. But stores need sufficient markup, and manufacturers will not produce enough merchandise for off-priced promotions in the face of controlled inventories. The alternative would be to concentrate largely on working with manufacturers to produce exclusive merchandise.

- The gasoline shortage may become more critical and could provide the rationale to intensify non-store merchandising: bill enclosures, mail and telephone ordering, and even radio and T.V., with the latter technique practiced, for the most part, by giant-sized firms.

- To ease consumer budget concerns, retailers will stress credit terms. Lay-aways and convenient payment plans will be incorporated into ads with greater frequency. Another tack could be widespread consumer opportunities to charge merchandise with delayed charge dates.

- Better priced stores, it is suspected, will continue to feature new styles at higher prices. This tactic can be utilized because the higher income consumer will be affected least by tight economic conditions.

- The competition for customer patronage was probably best exemplified by retail promotional efforts of the holiday period of 1979. Institutional ads featured such messages as: "You will be comfortable shopping in our store"; "Our store has the widest assortments of fashion"; "Our service is personalized," and "We are sensitive to fashion."

## 7. MERCHANDISING BY CLASSIFICATION

In an industry completely dependent upon ultimate consumer decision, there is constant search for styles that can be manufactured and sold successfully. The search is accompanied by producer awareness of the difficulty of assessing consumer purchase behavior with some degree of accuracy, and the fear of the inevitability of loss when merchandise is either out of trend or does not measure up to competition. Although these problems are common to all businesses in varying degrees, fashion producers are most vulnerable because of the industry's unique characteristics of the need to maintain a relatively rapid stock turn, the constancy of obsolescence and the minor importance of fashion merchandise's intrinsic value to consumers.

As a consequence of the inability of many firms to create and maintain a reasonable equilibrium between fashion demand and

*Planning*

goods produced, coupled with undercapitalization, the industry has the unenviable record of far exceeding the national business failure rate.

Pressure to hold a tigh reign on inventory has never been greater than in the current business climate. With the uncertainty of business conditions, reduced profitability, unprecedented cost of money and the relentless tide of imports, manufacturers are forced to exercise extreme effort to work with "lean" inventories and maximize return on investment. In more critical terms, survival well may depend upon the ability to accelerate stock turnover and minimize production of marginally-accepted styles.

Projecting and producing an ideally balanced inventory is almost an impossibility. A model stock is a goal, not a practical expectancy in a business that requires stock preparation and delivery of consumer wants of styles, colors and sizes. When deliveries are made early and complete, there is likelihood of overproduction.

Manufacturers traditionally control inventory levels by collating orders, putting into work styles of best buyer support and discarding poor sellers. This time-tested method is logical and works rather effectively. Inventory dislocations do develop, however, particularly when production includes anticipated reorders that do not occur and when "early bloomers abort on the retail vine," miscalculations by both store buyers and manufacturers. And in the natural course of events, overages are sold at promotional prices, not infrequently below cost, the effect of which is profit erosion. Obviously, with the current prime interest rate hovering about 20 percent (some economists predict the possibility of a rise to 28 percent), there is a mandate to maintain a healthy and profitable stock.

There is no originality in expressing the business objective to use capital to best advantage. And factually, there is no system that is infallible or guarantees to safeguard capital by preventing overproduction or the production of incorrect styles. But there is a method used by a related fashion industry sector that lessens the incidences of producing non-productive styles and promotes concentration on the "heart" of consumer demand. Manufacturers can take a leaf out of the book of sophisticated retailers who merchandise by classification, a system that helps to turn dollars into classes of wanted goods with reasonable accuracy, highlights fashion trends, avoids duplication of goods and maximizes capital usage. In essence, merchandising by classification is based on the concept that a classification is a unit of consumer demand, a *group of merchandise reasonably interchangeable from a customer's point of view.*

From the outset, it is recognized that retailers have an advantage over manufacturers. When a retailer's stock is not in consumer demand, there is usually sufficient time to correct omissions with additional purchases. But a manufacturer does not enjoy the luxury of time to make a turn-about, and the probable consequence is a "lost" season. The exception is the popular-price maker who "knocks-off" and adds styles on a more or less continuous basis.

The successful implementation of the system hinges on two basic marketing precepts. First, there must be conceptualization of why potential customers (end-users) should buy an organization's products—perhaps an oversimplification. Although this is neither the time nor the place to discuss the subjective subject of why customers buy apparel, it can be said that clothing as a highly personal product helps to accommodate group standards, offers the means to improve on natural endowment, evidences an effort to express self-concept, and in general, abets the aim to reach a state of betterment. It is apparent that styles must be designed to be somewhat more than decorative. The second fundamental is the need to identify and to make customers of retail stores that have the patronage of end-users for whom a firm's products have the greatest potential acceptance.

*Merchandise must be properly positioned to achieve the selling results it deserves.*

Once having targeted the two customer segments, the scene is set for the next stage, a plan that includes a realistic unit and dollar estimate of sales for the period of operation. The previous like-period's record is used as a base and then adjusted by applying the estimated effect of anticipated or planned factors such as: the economic situation, increased sales promotion events, new competitive forces, strengthened or increased sales staff, and above all, market strength based on fashion newness. In retailing, this planning is part of quantitative and qualitative control systems.

The next step is the key element. By reason of research, merchandise that is reasonably interchangeable is grouped and rated according to estimated importance for the period of operation.For example, a sportswear manufacturer after having digested foreign market reports, spoken to textile sources, held rap sessions with customers of importance to the firm, and collected data from other professional sources, could estimate the relative importance of classifications as:

| | |
|---|---|
| blazers | 15% |
| skirts | 25% |
| pants | 15% |
| blouses | 30% |
| sweaters | 15% |

These figures represent the planned investment in broad groups of consumer demand. The next step is to structure each classification with subclassifications—narrowed units of customer demand—styles that properly belong in the classifications. As a case in point, two

*Planning*

blazer subclassifications could be single- and double-breasted models.

By first grouping merchandise in broad terms and then "building" narrowed elements into them, a logically structured system is developed that assures the best reasons for production and capital usage because:

1. Each classification's investment is made after its importance is rated to other merchandise groups.
2. Each classification's production is allocated by dollars and units based on its importance to a fashion trend.
3. Subclassifications are *held to a minimum* since each style is selected when it has been proven as a necessary narrow unit of customer demand. Multiple styles within classifications are carried only when they are necessary as a condition of sale.

In using the merchandising by classification system, a manufacturer has a matrix that insures to the greatest degree: clearly defined reasons for the line inclusion of every style offered for sale, a reduction of line size, the production of fewer numbers in greater depth, and the best use of time, effort and capital.

As part of the consideration of improvising a system used by retailers, it is necessary to understand that the fundamental role of a store buyer is that of a selector, an agent of ultimate consumers. A buyer's responsibility is to purchase a narrow range of merchandise in in-trend classifications and subclassifications. Retailers who violate this principle by buying what looks good and practice "scatter" merchandising are doomed to failure. By applying the same rationale, manufacturers can narrow their range of styles so that each style represents a fashion point of view. "Watering" a line is evidence of indecision or weakness. In the final analysis, with few exceptions for specialty items, customers have limited fashion brand loyalty, consumers are prone to be motivated by what styles can "do" for them. If a customer wants a blue blazer, for example, the rigidity is in the demands of the color, silhouette and fit. A given manufacturer, a specific style, and to a degree, the details are variable factors of purchase terms.

It is ironic that manufacturers and retailers have been practicing merchandising by classification because of the importance of denim jeans. One style, predominantly in one color, with slight variation in details that "captured" the international market is a circumstance that would be hard to repeat. The fact is, however, blue denim jeans represent the extreme of merchandising by classification—narrowing stock to a specific demand.

Despite consumer capriciousness and the uncertainty of being able to accurately assess future best selling styles with any systematic approach, merchandising by classification is a way to rationalize what

*Strategies and Tactics in Fashion Marketing*

should be produced, in what quantities, and insure the most judicious use of capital.

As improvisations of the retail method of classification planning, figures 1 and 2 are techniques of recording planned and actual figures for the purposes of inventory analysis and control.

It can be seen that the collected information has the following advantages:

1. Perpetual inventory in units and colors.
2. Selling rate of each classification and subclassification.
3. Comparison between planned and actual figures.
4. Provision for revision of figures.
5. Base for future planning.
6. Identification of broad and narrow selling trends.

The recorded information is in compact form, easily accessible and requires little or no extra cost or effort. It can be maintained by

FIGURE 1

## CLASSIFICATION RECAPITULATION OF BLAZERS*

|  | UNITS | DOLLARS |  |
|---|---|---|---|
| Planned Sales (for season) | 19000 | 200,000 | 15 % of total Planned Sales (all classifications) |
| Adjusted Sales (for season) | 12,000 | 240,000 | 18 % of total Planned Sales (all classifications) |

UNITS

On hand __6,000__

In production __4,000__

Total commitment __10,000__

Orders to date __850__

Inventory to sell __9,150__    __7__ % of Planned Sales (for season)

__76__ % of Planned Production (for season)

Total units sold this week __850__

Weeks to sell __8__

*All styles

*Planning*

FIGURE 2 (Note each style is recorded on its own card sheet)

### SUBCLASSIFICATION SUMMARY

**Blazer**

Style #1500—Single-breasted—Gold buttons
In Units

| | INVENTORY | | | SALES | | |
|---|---|---|---|---|---|---|
| Week | In Production | In Stock | Total Commitment | Color | Total Sales | To Sell |
| 8/28 | 1,000 | 4,000 | 5,000 | White 100<br>Blue 250<br>Red 50 | 400 | 4,600 |

a hand-collated or computer based method. It is probable that most manufacturers maintain records of the same information, but with variances of rationale and technique.

Focusing on a narrowed but in greater depth range of styles may be the alternative to counteract the relentless pressures exerted on apparel producers. Merchandising by classification could be the alternative to maintain a streamlined liquid stock that in turn could help maintain fiscal liquidity.

## 8. CONSUMER RESEARCH

### Introduction

Every decision should be based on logic—on data that are presumed to be correct. Indeed, marketing decisions require highly accurate information because inaccurate assessments can lead to incorrect investments and major business dislocations.

Since one of the most important business concerns is the behavior of customers, marketers must find some way to obtain information about customer behavior that can be the basis for reasonable decisions for what to make, when to make it, at what prices, and in what quantities.

The subject of this text is the reasons for consumers' product decisions as a part of marketing. This chapter discusses consumer research—the methods and reasons for gathering information that can logically lead to marketing decisions about customers.

## Background and Definition

Marketing research was started in the early 1900's by the Curtis Publishing Company. A few years later, in 1915, Dr. Paul. H. Nystrom was employed by the United States Rubber Company to head up a research program. In 1919, Dr. C. S. Duncan wrote *Commercial Research—An Outline of Working Principles,* the first recognized book on the subject. Also, around 1920 the Department of Labor, in an effort to determine labor statistics for Congress preparatory to the enactment of minimum wage laws, needed consumer information; at the same time, unions initiated research to determine living costs preparatory to arbitration for increased wages.

Research assumed deeper meaning for industry following World War II. Marketers found themselves with products that were similar in appearance and price. Therefore, customers with more than adequate choices had to be studied to determine why, what, and how to produce goods that would satisfy them. This was the period that led to the era of "consumer orientation."

In the 1960's and 1970's, the importance of consumer research steadily increased because of the tremendous growth of business activity, dramatic changes in consumer characteristics (population, social values, education, and so on), new high levels of income, and unprecedented technological breakthroughs. Large business organizations realized that decision makers are often removed from direct contact with consumers and depend on records and other impersonal sources of information.

Present research need is not confined to the executives of giant organizations because conditions are essentially the same at every business level. The business environment requires supportive consumer information for proper decision making. The elements that are different are the dimension of the marketing problem or opportunity and the depth of research need.

In general, marketing research objectives are as follows:

1. To identify a marketing opportunity or problem
2. To isolate the problem and other issues
3. To evaluate alternatives for the problem
4. To select an alternative to "solve" the problem
5. To implement strategies and tactics into marketing practices to fulfill the objectives

Consumer research as part of marketing, therefore, is specifically directed toward determining the nature and characteristics of consumers as individuals and groups.

## Specific Problems for Research

Although the specific reasons for consumer research are too numerous to mention, the following is a list of the most common purposes for it.

1. Nature of markets
   a. Locate customer
   b. Characterize customer
   c. Change customer
   d. Compare market
   e. Determine market potential
   f. Estimate sales
2. Motivation
   a. Analyze motives for purchase
   b. Establish factors influencing motives
   c. Establish motives behind product and store preferences
   d. Analyze motives for shopping and comparing products
3. Attitudes
   a. Establish attitude toward store
   b. Establish attitude toward product brand
   c. Determine problems of consumer dissatisfaction
   d. Analyze relative strength of attitudes
   e. Determine store image
   f. Determine product image
   g. Analyze attitude toward distance traveled to shop
   h. Evaluate attitude toward purchase planning
4. Preference
   a. Determine store preferences
   b. Determine product preferences
   c. Estimate store loyalty
   d. Estimate product loyalty
   e. Establish trade area preferences
   f. Determine purchase frequency
5. Intentions
   a. Estimate purchase intentions
   b. Analyze relationships between aspirations and purchase intent
   c. Determine degree of intent realization

## Research Considerations

The easiest research involves demographics because statistics are relatively easy to obtain. In fact, income levels are often used as the main ingredient for marketing conclusions. The more difficult data are the opinions, attitudes, and beliefs of consumers (psychographics), generally referred to as *predispositions*. Since this term has several meanings, it is well to define its three qualitative connotations:

- *Attitude* is usually defined as action tendencies.
- *Opinions* are verbal responses to questions.

*Strategies and Tactics in Fashion Marketing*

- *Beliefs* are connected with cultural and social backgrounds, such as religious and political convictions.

Marketing practice should make use of both demographic and psychographic information, especially since the rise in business activity requires the most incisive consumer information. Income levels, although easily available, cannot be the sole standard for predicting or understanding consumer behavior.

## Research Procedures

Research starts with a clear statement of what information is required about consumers so that applicable data may be gathered and analyzed. Although research procedures vary according to the problem need, the following steps are inclusive but flexible.

1. Define objectives and problem
2. Plan the investigation
    a. Determine sources of information
    b. Determine methods of gathering data
    c. Prepare data gathering forms
    d. Prepare questionnaire (when surveys are needed)
    e. Plan the sample (people to be involved, how many, of what characteristics)
    f. Collect the data
3. Tabulate and analyze the data
4. Interpret the data and prepare a written report
5. Follow up to ensure efficiency of research

Once the identification of a customer opportunity or problem is determined, a study is made to establish the cost of the project and to determine how facts can best be gathered. Information can be collected from either primary or secondary sources. With the former, data are obtained directly from the source, tailored to the project. Surveys can be made by personal interview, mail, or telephone. With secondary sources, data are secured from information collected from various sources. Secondary data can be obtained internally from company records such as invoices, salespersons' earning reports, shipments, returns, unit control, markdowns, financial reports, and credit department data. The selected data should answer positively: Does the information apply to the need? Is the information sufficiently current to be meaningful to the problem?

The type of source used depends only on the circumstances. In some instances, both types are employed. There is an abundance of sources; these include the following:

1. Federal, state and local government
    a. Census data (U.S. Bureau of Census)
    b. Registration data (government agencies) about births, deaths, marriages, school enrollment, income tax returns, social security payments, and the like
2. Colleges and universities

*Planning*

3. Foundations
4. Professional associations
5. Trade associations
6. Chambers of commerce
7. Publishing companies
8. Commercial organizations

Selected statistical works should include the following sources of information:

1. Board of Governors, Federal Reserve System. *Federal Reserve Bulletin.* Washington, D.C. Monthly. Includes statistics in retailing.
2. Standard and Poor's Corporation. *Standard and Poor's Trade and Securities.* New York. Monthly.
3. U.S. Bureau of Labor Statistics, Department of Labor. *Monthly Labor Review.* Washington, D.C. Monthly.
4. U.S. Bureau of the Census. *Statistical Abstract of the United States.* Washington, D.C. Annual.
5. U.S. Internal Revenue Service, Department of the Treasury. *Statistics of Income.* Washington, D.C. Annual.
6. The Conference Board, "A Guide to Consumer Markets." New York. Annual.

## Basic Methods of Collecting Data

The primary requirement of research is that the collected information be accurate if it is to achieve useful results. Too often researchers are carried away with their own predispositions, influencing an interview to conform to their ideas or deliberately collecting information that supports their desired results. This leads to the research acronym GIGO—"garbage in, garbage out." Computer print-out information, for example, is only as good as the data put into the computer. Research can be brief, simple, and uncomplicated as long as it ensures the required data.

Research employs three basic methods: the experimental method, the survey method, and the observational method.

**Experimental Method.** The experimental method involves tailoring a scale model (mockup structure) or controlled experiment. The value of a scale model is based on the assumption that what happens in a model situation will probably happen proportionately in a larger situation. For example, a retail buyer stocks twelve pieces of a style to test the rate of sale. If most or all sell immediately, the buyer has evidence that the style will probably continue to sell well (proportionately) when stocked in greater quantity. It could be evidence of suitability for a sales promotion to generate high volume selling.

*Strategies and Tactics in Fashion Marketing*

A controlled experiment involves establishing a control market. For example, the retail buyer stocks the same style of garment in different stores, *with one variable*—one branch store stocked with two colors not available in the other stores. The selling results of all stores should reveal the relative importance of color to the garment's selling rate. A buyer can use the variable in deciding how best to merchandise goods (and in deciding the importance of that variable to total sales).

**Survey Method.** The survey method, widely used in gathering data, involves interviewing a limited number of people (sample group) selected from a large group. Parenthetically, the term *microcosm* should be introduced at this time. The term means a miniature of the whole; for example, the city of Syracuse could be the microcosm for a study of city people. The assumption is that the value system of people in this metropolis is considered typical of the people in an average city of the United States.

The advantage of the survey method is that the original source of information is reached—that is, the people whose motives, opinions, attitudes, and beliefs about buying are being researched. Its inherent weakness is that respondents often give false or inadequate information. For this reason, carefully planned questionnaires and anticipation by seasoned researchers are required. Different wording of questions frequently results in different responses.

**Observational Method.** The relatively uncomplicated observational method can be narrowed down to two types:

1. Collection of data by observing objects or actions—for example, in weighing the possible location of a store, standing on the corner and taking a head count of passersby' to determine potential customer traffic.
2. Observation of collected data, as described earlier in this chapter in the section on research procedures (pp. 40–41).

**Summary of Methods.** The particular method to be used must be related to the time the research requires, the money it will cost, the personnel available, and the facilities available to implement the research. Whereas the survey method is probably most commonly used, there seems to be a growing trend toward using the other two. A survey is a process that is complicated by many built-in moot areas. In fashion marketing the observational and experimental methods are by far the most important.

## Limitations of Research

Although consumer research is an exceedingly important management tool, it is not a complete answer to all problems. It eliminates impressions and hunches, but it does have limitations, which can lead to incorrect conculsions. Research failure may result from any of the following:

1. Inadequately trained personnel.
2. Bias on the part of researchers who use data to support prejudices.
3. The fact that research is a social science with no precise formulas or theorems (effective conclusions are based on good judgment).
4. The fact that objectives can be in conflict—management must have a clear understanding that all participants are willing to support a common objective.

Despite extensive research and millions of dollars of promotional support, 60 percent of all products put on the market result in marketing failure. *Research does not solve problems; it presents data on which executive judgment can be logically based.*

## Consumer Research and Fashion Marketing Uniqueness

Some people claim that the fashion business is the "Wild West of industry" because it is volatile and never allows the practitioner to rest on past laurels. Today's success is tomorrow's failure. What one has done lately is the concern, and lately is today.

There are many reasons why this endeavor is unique and requires different business techniques and understanding of ultimate customer decisions. Some of the "problems" may be identified as acceptance and people, time, and place.

**Acceptance and People.** Fashion apparel is a special product, one that is personal, reflects an attitude, and has a variety of meanings to customers. The satisfaction one derives from clothing depends on many things, including one's lifestyle and age, income, peer group and family, status values, education, cultural group, sex (of course), and profession.

One might say that almost all products are affected by these influences. However, there is a difference of degree because of the nature of apparel, which is a conspicuous, personal-purchase product. Clothing as a reflection of attitude states:

- This is who I am.
- This is what I would like to be.

- This is how I would like people to think of me.
- This is how I believe people think of me.

Which reflection is most important at a given time is as variable as people themselves, and it is the crux of our discussion. If we agree that fashion has four elements—*acceptance, people, time,* and *place*—we realize the complications of marketing this unique product.

Acceptance implies that the final judge is the consumer, and that is the main fact of fashion life. A fashion, therefore, is the "winner" of a democratic process whereby the producer nominates and the consumer elects. The number of votes it takes to win an election is variable; it depends on whether the fashion is limited (one for a small group of people) or broad (one meant for many people). The key word is *substantial,* which has a quantitative meaning. A producer has to make a choice as to what segment of the market is to be served. If the segmentation is people with high income, *substantial* may mean a potential audience of thousands. If *substantial* is equated with millions of people, the segmentation is broad and common-denominator merchandise is the focus. A couture dressmaker may have a $3-million volume per annum and be considered highly successful, but a popular-priced maker doing the same volume would be considered a producer of small market significance.

From the most general viewpoint, acceptance is based on the consumer's desire to better himself or herself, which is the reason for any purchase. What is "better" depends on who the customer is or what the customer wants to be.

One of the unique characteristics of acceptance is that it includes negation. When something new is accepted, there is a rejection of the old. The marketer is cognizant of this and overtly attempts to speed up this negation by seasonally offering a new product that differs from what is owned already by the customer. If the selling is a success, the consumer will reject what is presently owned in favor of the newer item, even though the old has utility value. *This is the heart of fashion.* When the newness has great acceptance and thereby "ages" what was the fashion, the fashion business is at its healthiest.

This sounds easy to do but it is not. Customers do not like abrupt changes that invalidate ownership; the eye and mind reject ideas that negate what is comfortable and understood. Therefore, fashion must evolve gradually. For example, recall the trend to shorter hemlines; it took five years for hemlines to go from mid-calf to the knees.

A basic principle of fashion is that acceptance is evolutionary. The diffusion of new products can be exemplified best by the follow-

*Planning*

ing estimation of the percentage of people who accept new products and when.

| | |
|---|---|
| Innovators | 2.5 percent |
| Early accepters | 13.5 |
| Early majority | 34 |
| Late majority | 34 |
| Laggards | 16 |
| | 100 percent |

Two complications have been discussed in this section—*acceptance* and *people*, who are often fickle and capricious in their choices but who in the final analysis, know what they want when they see it. The producer's problem is to recognize the signs and to produce goods in line with probable customer preferences. Unfortunately, keeping pace with wanted consumer satisfactions is a hard task and one of the major problems of fashion marketing.

**Time.** Time is a major problem because the fashion year can consist of up to six seasons, each requiring new merchandise. Producing six hit fashion shows a year is extremely difficult. Not every maker, however, is concerned with six periods. The retailer must feature merchandise of all seasons of interest to the segmented audience. A store selling high-priced merchandise observes all the seasons; a low-priced store concentrates on the conventional seasons: spring, summer, fall, and winter (holiday).

The seasonality of fashion is related to obsolescence. That which is new has the best chance of selling in the greatest quantities; that which is old has a limited market potential and must be marked down to establish a new appeal—low price.

This leads to another problem (or principle) of fashion—change. A healthy stock condition for any producer is new versions of acceptable merchandise. Age is related to low prices, merchandise suitable for laggards, and used up (obsolete) merchandise, even though the obsolescence is psychological. The penalty for being late in fashion marketing is to be left with one appeal—"I have it at a cheaper price." (The term *producer* is used here in the sense that anyone who is not a consumer is a producer, so there is interchangeable reference to textile producers, manufacturers of finished products, and retailers as producers.)

**Place.** Cultural and subcultural values are important influences on the degree of acceptance. Climate, ethnic styles, and regional attitudes are marketing concerns. This factor is a complicated one for a producer who seeks a national market; obviously, different styles, colors, and fabrics must be incorporated in a collection or stock to accommodate different regions and/or groups who have their own views about the meaning of fashion.

## A Summary of Fashion Marketing Uniqueness

The textile, manufacturing, and retail markets constantly wrestle with one common objective—how to determine customer preference at a given time. The lack of precise research techniques to accommodate relatively rapid fashion changes is the rationale for some critics naming the business "The Rat Race."

The following is a listing of the major "problems" or considerations for marketers:

1. The inherent element of psychological obsolescence.
2. Low intrinsic value relationship.
3. The seasonality of fashion.
4. The condition of change, which also brings high markdowns and the need for fast turnover of stock.
5. A business based on emotional responses requires dramatic sales promotion.
6. The business includes:
    a. High level of competition.
    b. Relatively small investment needed to enter business (for manufacturers); the "game" is for manufacturers to maintain a high level of sales, often using contractors instead of owning machinery.
    c. The accepted practice of "stealing" or copying the styles of others ("knocking-off").

## Consumer Research in the Fashion Markets

**The Textile Market.** The earliest research for the fashion of the season starts in this sector because its products (fibers and fabrics) must accommodate manufacturers who place orders from two to six months before they show lines to retailers. This market enjoys several advantages:

1. Many industry leaders are large enough to afford research facilities.
2. Selling volume is sufficiently high to permit long-term planning; efforts need not bring immediate results.
3. Research budgets include the use of specialists in areas of importance.

Chemical companies, as part of fashion marketing, maintain research and development programs in polymer chemistry for the development of synthetic fabrics. In addition, they have marketing representatives who become experts in the fashion trends of both Europe and America. Studies usually start on the European continent because that part of the world is in the fashion foreground; styles are developed and accepted by customers in Europe before they are in America. The experts inspect couture merchandise, retail stores, prêt-à-porter offerings, and people. The research objectives are the trends of silhouette, color, texture, and details—necessary information for firms that must accommodate manufacturers with one of the main ingredients of styles, the fabric.

This research is done so that textile firms can plan and/or develop lines up to a year before the manufacturers show their lines to buyers. Once research is completed, the composition of the new line is decided by stylists and executives.

Since the advent of man-made fabrics there has been an intensification of research efforts; research is a necessary function of the chemical company. In fact, the chemical industry is a leader in research efforts to determine consumer motivation. Chemical companies are well aware that man-made fibers play an important part in everyone's life, and once a strong brand name is established, they know it has the potential to add millions of dollars to their sales volume through the marketing of their other products. Hence, consumer research in the textile section is professionally based, widely practiced, and heavily invested.

Textile companies use all three basic methods of research, with surveys usually confined to their own customers, the manufacturers, who are able to give well-defined sales figures and purchase plans as well as the reasons for them. These plans are based on manufacturers' past records and their own research efforts. As an example of this research pattern, one of the largest textile firms in the United States, which grosses over $1 billion a year, does 80 percent of its volume with 110 accounts. Six to eight months before scheduled market deliveries, the firm surveys these important customers to learn their intentions. The information gathered is used as the basis for a sales forecast and, therefore, for initial production levels. This practice enables the textile firm to predict, within reasonable limits, the business activity in advance of the season.

The experimental method is widely used in setting up pilot situations for newly developed yarns and/or fabrics. As examples, when Nylon and Orlon were being introduced, Du Pont maintained low levels of production and limited distribution to selected manufacturers in different areas of apparel manufacturing. Hence, variables were set up from which Du Pont was able to glean sufficient information about the reaction of the fiber on the cutting table of manufacturers, manufacturers' opinions of the fabrics, and most important of all, the feedback from ultimate consumers about a variety of finished apparel.

Observational research is another widely practiced method. Retail stock movement, internal records, couture merchandise acceptance, and end users are observed by professionals.

A big investment of time and money in long production goods necessitates research—without it the wheels of production could not turn.

**The Manufacturer.** In the fashion industry the manufacturers are characterized by small firms, the practice of "knocking-off," and goods produced on a seasonal basis.

If there is a weak link in the chain of the fashion flow of apparel dynamics, it is the manufacturing sector. In the manufacturing of female apparel, the attrition rate is about 17 percent per annum, making the average life of a manufacturer approximately six years. The problems of fashion marketing previously described are inherent for life of all manufacturers. One additional factor was implied but not stated specifically. Since high capital investment is not a necessary condition of going into business, the idea of being in business for oneself lures salespeople and production workers to open their own establishments. In due time, undercapitalization and inability to discern customer wants results in failure for many.

The vast majority of apparel makers lean heavily on speaking to textile executives, retail buyers, and noncompetitive manufacturers. Since most manufacturers are imitators or copyists (the nature of the business), they wait for higher-priced manufacturers to disclose their lines and then imitate them at lower prices.

Higher-priced firms watch European markets for general trends and then develop their own versions for the American market. A small sector, the couture area, creates originals, as do the French and Italian creators. Although markets differ, the creative approach depends on the sensitivity of the designer to the influences of the times.

Only the few large manufacturers occasionally employ specialists to do formal research surveys to discern customer attitudes for the purpose of establishing new products or investing heavily in certain classifications of merchandise. (Such research efforts are illustrated later in this chapter.) On some occasions, large firms have used the experimental method—for example, delivering hosiery simultaneously to selected department stores and to supermarkets to determine whether the merchandise should be marketed like detergent, stocking and filling in merchandise as needed from store reserve stock. This interesting marketing technique could be a wave of the future.

*Planning*

Manufacturers as a group, therefore, do informal research by studying their own records, speaking to other levels of the industry, subscribing to foreign fashion magazines, subscribing to color associations (foreign and domestic), and examining store stocks.

Research is done continuously, and its conclusions, it is to be hoped, lead to the production of styles that have greatest consumer acceptance in the selected channels of distribution. The high-priced market needs the information earliest, the moderate market later, and the popular-priced level latest, because fashion development and required retail stock demands it—highest priced merchandise sells earliest.

**The Retailer.** The nature of retailing is unique in the marketing practice because it is the one area where the buyer/seller relation is initiated by the consumer. Fundamentally, the patronage motives are overt and can be supported by company records.

Although most large stores have research bureaus, their main interest is retail efficiency areas such as those concerning store layout designs, customer traffic studies, operation systems, and other broad areas of retail concern. They do develop population studies and income studies and in a general way research group customer preference.

The responsibility for selecting the specific merchandise for customer approval, however, falls to the buyer, the agent for the ultimate customer. The buyer uses all three methods of research. The survey method is done informally by questioning customers about their intentions on the selling floor. However, the large store buyer has limited time for this important research method. So buyers should, and do, survey the "soldiers" of selling, the salespeople, who can be valuable interviewers.

The buyer has more sources of information to predict consumer demand than any other person involved in fashion merchandising. As stated, a big advantage is the interrelationship of the end-user with those who are in the "line of fire." Here is a list of observation sources, widely available to all buyers:

1. Sales records—by units, dollars, and classifications (These department records are used to determine past and future customer demands.)
2. Trends in related departments
3. Resident buying reports—the buyer's eyes, ears, and legs in the market
4. Trade publications
5. Fashion magazines
6. Data from competing stores (including ads)

7. Fashion coordinators' reports
8. Observing people in their daily activities
9. Data from associated stores
10. Buyers' records—diaries of past events
11. Fashion shows
12. Market trips—reviewing manufacturers' lines and narrowing merchandise into groups (classification) of most importance to the potential customers of the department

Many of these sources can also be used with the survey method, without a formal questionnaire. The buyer has objectives, the selection of merchandise that accommodates the department's needs, and therefore will question manufacturers, textile people (on occasion), sales personnel (as stated), resident buyers, and fashion coordinators (of store and resident buying office).

The controlled experiment is constantly used to guide the buyer. Once merchandise is put in stock, it is evaluated for its sales potential. The buyer has a record of the date of receipt, quantity received, customers' preference of colors, sizes, and level of acceptance. With this information the buyer must evaluate future demand and act accordingly. Since there are the additional factors of seasonality, "knock-offs" at lower prices, and newer market developments, the course of action can be reordering for replacement, promoting to accelerate sales, or dropping in favor of a new style. This is the professional requirement for a buyer.

## 9. INCOME AND EXPENDITURES

### Importance and Definition of Income

A well-run family, business, or government is deeply concerned with income, which establishes the ability to purchase goods and services. Income is of such importance that many use it as the sole criterion for segmenting a market—establishing groups by income levels, even using income to measure status level. It is a fundamental principle that a marketer must assess market importance to numbers of people and assess both their ability and their willingness to buy.

The ability to buy depends on the availability of income, which has several meanings.

*Personal income* is the total of wages and salaries, including proprietary and rental income, interest, dividends, and transfer payments. It does not include capital gains or losses. Transfer payments are receipts from government and business for which no services are rendered, government payments and corporate gifts to nonprofit institutions, and individuals' bad debts to business.

*Disposable income* is the net or remaining income after deduc-

*Planning*

tion of personal tax and other payments (fines and penalties) to general government.

*Discretionary or supernumerary* (The Conference Board defines supernumerary income as the amount in excess of $20,000 a year for a family unit.) income refers to that share of income which is not needed for essentials and is available for optional spending.

*Subsistence income* is the amount of money needed to cover the necessities of life.

The following identifies various types of income and allocation of income by the average urban family of four.

| | | | |
|---|---|---|---|
| Personal income ($10,064) | | | 100 percent |
| Personal taxes | | | −17 percent |
| Disposable income | | | 83 percent |
| Necessities: | Food | 23 percent | |
| | Housing | 24 percent | |
| | Transportation | 9 percent | |
| | Clothing | 9 percent | |
| | Personal and medical care | 5 percent | |
| | Occupational costs | 1 percent | −71 percent |
| Discretionary income | | | 12 percent |
| Family recreation | | 6 percent | |
| Savings, gifts, and contributions | | 6 percent | −12 percent |
| | | | 0 |

## Income—The Ability to Buy

The current yearly gross national product (GNP) of the United States is in excess of $1.5 trillion, by far exceeding that of any other country. It therefore follows that we have the greatest ability to buy both the necessities and luxuries of life.

The average American lives more comfortably than did kings or despots in their heydays. It would have been beyond their imagination to think of homes with central and controlled temperature, means of transportation (autos, planes, and so on), the varieties of foods available to the average American, entertainment in the home (radio, T.V., hi-fi, and the like), and clothing of an infinite variety (washable, durable, crease resistant, and so on).

Department of Commerce figures for 1974 clearly establish why the average American can "luxuriate" far beyond most people of the world. They also explain marketers' potential in the land of plenty.

>Total personal income: $1,148,720,000,000
>Median family income: $12,051
>Percentage of families with an income of $10,000 or more: 64.5 percent
>Per capita income: $5,434

The following chart from the same source exhibits the shifting power of consumption and indicates a healthier economic state for many people.

### The Changing Income Pyramid
*Total families each year—100%; based on 1973 dollars*

| 1963 | Income Class | 1973 |
|---|---|---|
| 18.3% | $15,000 and over | 35.5% |
| 25.2% | 10,000–15,000 | 25.5% |
| 21.7% | 7,000–10,000 | 14.9% |
| 12.1% | 5,000–7,000 | 9.4% |
| 11.6% | 3,000–5,000 | 8.6% |
| 11.2% | under 3,000 | 6.0% |

If one were to graph these figures, 1963 could almost be shown as a pyramid, with the greatest number of families in the group from $10,000 and below. By 1973 the pyramid was turned around 180°, with most American families in the group earning $10,000 or over.

Demographers present a bright future for the last few years of the seventies, with some characterizing them as the era of exploding affluence. Others, however, would say, with justification, that inflation has eroded purchasing power, and the significance of $10,000 a year as earnings has diminished. Also, people with higher incomes have had to adjust their purchase priorities in favor of the necessities of life.

As families climb the ladder of affluence, they obtain the power to buy those things that help make life more pleasant, discretionary products—luxuries of today that the "folks" will own tomorrow.

It is almost amusing to note what could have been characterized as products owned by the Joneses of yesterday that have become commonplace today. Just imagine that the following products were luxury products of yesterday (circa 1920): an automobile, a sewing machine, a telephone, a refrigerator.

One of the factors contributing to the growth of income is unionism. Because of union pressure, wages have increased to a point where blue collar workers such as carpenters, electricians, plumbers, and truck drivers, and local government workers such as police and firefighters make more in annual wages than white collar workers including professionals. It is not uncommon for a union plumber to earn a great deal more than a veteran high school teacher.

These are reasons why Americans can indulge in so many fancies and can reject presently owned products in favor of new ones, even though the old are still useful. Is there any other way to describe the American attitude about the fashion of products—particularly fashion apparel?

Lest the reader consider the authors insensitive to the eternal problem of maldistribution of wealth, let us add that there is an inequitable diffusion of income in the United States. It is generally held that there are about 25 million people living at the poverty level. The prevailing poverty threshold figure is $5,000 per annum for a nonfarm family of four persons, of whom 27 percent are under twenty-five years of age and 26 percent are over 65 (a group that is increasing at an unprecedented pace). There are approximately 9 million nonwhite and 16 million white persons in such families. These are depressing facts in the land of plenty—12 percent of the population living at a substandard level. Naturally, their purchasing power is limited and mitigates against the economic health of the country—not to mention how it affects the psyche and social abilities of the victims, grownups and children.

## What Is Bought

The simplest reason for purchasing any goods is the desire to reach a state of betterment. Marketing scholars could say that consumers seek to maximize their satisfactions. At this point we can discuss the law of diminishing marginal utility, which says that consumers derive decreasing enjoyment from the continual purchase of additional goods. As an example, a young man buys a tailored suit after having been in jeans for a good part of his life. The first suit purchased will probably give him the greatest pleasure and utility. If a second suit is purchased, it affords a choice of outfit, but doesn't provide the same degree of pleasure. The third suit will give still less pleasure, the fourth still less, and additional suits, although having some value, will give decreasing satisfaction. The biggest thrill was in the possession of the first.

One of the realities of life is that it takes money to buy anything, and those who have more of it can buy more products and services at higher prices, and with greater frequency. As a common sense principle, as prices go up sales are inhibited because fewer people are able or want to buy products at those levels. Even if one can afford certain products, value is compared to price. From a marketing point of view, when the customer equates price and value, or when the value is greater than the price, there is affirmative action, the product is purchased. When there is a reverse situation, the result is price resistance, the refusal to buy. What is value is a complicated subject. It brings to mind the cost of a leather jacket that was displayed in a popular-priced store in New York at $90. As an interested viewer, the writer watched the young customers and tried to establish some theory as to why so many seventeen- to nineteen-year-olds bought it, where they got the money, and what was sacrificed to purchase it. This homily could be the subject of an in-depth discussion. The reader can enumerate many common examples. To cite one example of value versus price, how about the housewife who travels a great distance to buy the special, a loss leader, ketchup at nine cents a bottle, probably spending an hour or better, after she purchased most groceries in the local supermarket.

Another aspect of the relationship between income and purchases was developed in the middle nineteenth century by a government statistician named Ernst Engel. He supplied evidence of a well-known fact; poor people spend a larger share of their total income for food than do rich people; as income rises, the proportion spent for food declines.

Engel's theories became known as Engel's Laws and can be summarized as follows:

1. As income rises, the proportion spent on food declines.
2. As income rises, the proportion spent on housing and household goods remains about the same.
3. As income rises, the proportion spent on clothing stays the same or perhaps rises slightly.
4. As income rises, the proportion spent on luxuries rises.

Like most theories, the laws are sometimes bent and disregarded, but, in the main, they hold up pretty well and are considered valid after more than one hundred years. Note that the conclusions are based on proportion (percentage of income) and not total dollars.

In 1973 the Department of Commerce developed a pattern of average personal consumer spending:

| Type of Product | Percentage |
| --- | --- |
| Food, beverages, tobacco | 22.2 |
| Clothing | 10.1 |
| Clothing care | 1.5 |
| Personal care | 14.5 |
| Housing | 14.6 |
| Household operations | 7.8 |
| Medical care | 5.6 |
| Personal business | 13.6 |
| Transportation | 6.5 |
| Recreation | 1.6 |
| Private education, research | 1.3 |
| Religious, welfare activities | 1.3 |
| Foreign travel and other | .7 |

*Planning*

How people spend money depends to a great degree on the life cycle of the family. The following is based on a 1967 study by the National Conference Board of New York. It notes that families with older children spend relatively large amounts on food and clothing. Young families devote large shares to buying and furnishing a home.

|  | Total | Families with Child Under 6 |  | 6 or Over |  | No Children |  |
|---|---|---|---|---|---|---|---|
|  |  | Some Under 6 | All Under 6 | 6 to 11 | Age 12 & Over | Husband & Wife | Other |
| Food, beverage & tobacco | 29% | 30 | 26 | 28 | 28 | 27 | 28 |
| Housing & household operations | 24% | 24 | 27 | 24 | 21 | 25 | 30 |
| House furnishings & equipment | 5% | 5 | 6 | 5 | 5 | 5 | 4 |
| Clothing | 10% | 11 | 9 | 11 | 12 | 9 | 9 |
| Transportation | 14% | 13 | 17 | 15 | 15 | 16 | 12 |
| Medical & personal care | 10% | 9 | 9 | 9 | 9 | 11 | 10 |
| Recreation & equipment | 4% | 4 | 4 | 4 | 4 | 4 | 3 |
| Reading & education | 2% | 2 | 1 | 2 | 3 | 1 | 1 |
| Other goods & services | 2% | 2 | 1 | 2 | 3 | 2 | 2 |

## A Good Reason to Spend Money

The story is told of a man of sixty who was born in another country and arrived in the United States with his parents at the age of eight. The family established residence in the ghetto of New York. Life was hard and money scarce. The work ethic did not have to be explained to them; all their friends, relatives, and acquaintances were in the same boat—everyone worked his nails to the bone.

After a life of arduous labor and savings, the man had it made by American standards; he owned his own business and accumulated enough wealth to buy for his family and himself all the luxuries of life. The Horatio Alger story was followed in a classic manner.

When he was settled into a mansion on the North Shore of Long Island he invited his friends and relatives to a cocktail party that included gourmet food and a variety of liquors that spelled wealth. This was his "coming out" party.

One of his business associates was so impressed that he requested a full tour of the house and grounds. "My goodness," the visitor uttered, after entering each room, each having been decorated in the finest taste (naturally, by a famous interior designer).

Finally, they arrived on the back terrace overlooking a vast, well-manicured lawn surrounded by lovely shrubbery (landscaped by a well-known garden architect). It was a sight to behold!

After a few minutes of admiration, the visitor noted another house about two acres away. "Say," he said, "this house is magnificent, but look at that place, it looks like a place fit for a king."

"Oh," the host replied, "that is where my daughter and son-in-law reside."

"Your son-in-law?" inquired the guest. "What did he do to earn that house?"

"Well," the host replied, "he got four A's and one B."

## Income, Expenditures, and Fashion Apparel

**General Observations.** The percentage of disposable income spent on clothing has remained relatively constant through the years, roughly about 10 percent. According to the 1973 figures of the Department of Commerce, consumer spending at retail for apparel was as follows:

| | |
|---|---|
| Total | $81,274 billion |
| Men's and boys' | 20,835 |
| Women's and children's | 38,862 |
| Shoes, other footwear | 10,403 |
| Clothing care services | 6,172 |
| Jewelry and watches | 4,914 |

These figures are huge proportionally, about five percent of the total GNP. Since they are gross numbers, and include clothing for military personnel, clothing care, and watches, we can refine them to a net of about $70 billion, which will focus more nearly on the subject of our discussion—fashion apparel as purchased in retail stores. The ratio between men's and boys' and women's and children's is 35 to 65 respectively—a relationship that has remained constant. It would appear, despite the "peacock revolution," that male clothing is a delayed purchase. In order of priority, purchases are for children first, then Mama, and last and possibly least, for Papa. Could this be one of the last remnants of chauvinism on the part of the authors?

Income is undoubtedly one of the most important factors causing variation in customer demands for goods and services. Level of income determines to a great extent not only how much can be spent on goods but also what quality of merchandise will be purchased.

Marketers recognize that certain products or services are available for those with high incomes. For example, *The Wall Street Journal* could be one of the proper periodicals in which to advertise the sale or availability of yachts, airplanes, foreign trips, and other offerings that richer people can afford. And although clothing has been democratized, particularly in America, through mass production and man-made fabrics, apparel, particularly for females, is still the single most important product through which the wealthy can signal their position in society. So income can be related to purchasing patterns, except for blue-collar workers, who sometimes earn more than white-collar workers but who tend to spend income with the value system of their social rather than their income group.

**Fashion Marketing—Wholesale Markets.** The term *wholesale markets,* for this discussion, refers to the two sectors before the retailer: the textile suppliers and the manufacturers.

All three markets recognize that there are three price ranges to suit the pocketbooks of customers:

    The better market (highest prices)
    The moderate market (middle prices)
    The popular market (low prices)

Accordingly, each market concentrates on price levels that accommodate their segmented targets. The segmentation is most defined in the manufacturing sector, even to the extent of showroom locations. In New York, 7th Avenue is the couture or better area, Broadway the moderate area, and side streets are where the popular markets are located. Most textile firms, however, run the price gamut and not uncommonly have different departments, brands, and salespersons catering to manufacturers of different price levels.

What is fascinating is the development of merchandise at different price levels based on the need to accommodate different retail groups. Stores display and sell the highest priced items earliest, because customers with money can indulge their wants at will. The theory is that people with more money can and are able to buy earliest. Newness is often equated with higher costs. If one wants the new when it is available in relatively limited quantities, a price must be paid. People with less money buy lower priced items and tend to defer the date of purchase. Deferring the purchase date causes manufacturers and retailers to accommodate themselves to the needs of these people. Although some new fashion offerings are influenced by the young and therefore come at lower prices, creative designing by and large comes at high price levels.

Responding to the economic and psychological patterns of consumer spending and commercialism, the wholesale market offers its collections on the following calendar:

| Season | Better and Higher Priced | Moderate Priced | Popular Priced |
|---|---|---|---|
| Fall | April/May | June | October |
| Resort and Cruise | Sept. 15/Oct. Oct. 15/Nov. | Oct. 15/Nov. | Nov.* |
| Spring | January | Jan./Feb. | Mar./Apr.* |
| Summer | May | May/June | |
| Transition | | | |

*The start of showings with continuing style developments throughout the season.

The wholesalers study foreign and domestic markets with an eye on the broad influences affecting the market, not the least of which is the economic state at the time of the line development. Limited income, high taxes, and inflation are factors that lessen the ability of consumers to buy. The classification of fashion merchandise is affected by bad times—just how much depends on the priority of customer need. Following are a few examples of the effect periods of lower income have on fashion purchases.

In times of depression, there is relatively insignificant lowering of customers' ability to buy high-priced goods. The highest income customers are in stable economic circumstances and are least affected. Therefore, manufacturers are not adversely affected. Statistics prove that luxury items sold as well or better than usual during the recession of the seventies.

Moderate-priced clothing fares poorly during periods of recession. Females particularly, tend to buy components for newness, thereby spending the least amount of money to create a new outfit. It is less expensive to buy only a new sweater or blouse, for example. And the male of a family, in these times, may end up pressing his old suits, or buy only a component such as a jacket. A male s suit is often a delayed purchase anyway, one that is made after the rest of the family has been satisfied.

The wholesale market is deeply concerned about the state of economy because the level of business decreases in proportion to national income loss.

The popular-priced market in depressed times tends to gain support from those who are normally customers of moderate-priced markets and loses support from its regular customers who are reduced to a subsistence standard of living. In "good times" these popular-priced customers tend to move up to moderate levels. One of the problems encountered by some discount stores during the late 1960's and early 1970's was that popular-priced apparel did not have

*Planning*

sufficiently broad appeal, and most customers preferred quality merchandise. To this day, some discounters are having a difficult time selling fashion goods.

In depressed times manufacturers use ingenuity to buy fabrics and labor at reduced costs and offer promotional goods at advantageous retail levels. All the opportunistic practices of the business then come to the surface for survival.

The average life of a manufacturer is about six years, which is approximately a 17 percent annual attrition rate. Although the problem of ready-to-wear manufacturers is rooted in their inability to keep pace with customers' preferences, economic downturns also play a part in the fashion makers' dilemma. Again, the reduction of market size—potential—is directly related to income—the ability to buy.

**Fashion Marketing—Retailers.** The retail sector of fashion is certainly a stronger link in the fashion chain than the secondary level of fashion—the manufacturing area. But even in this sector failures occur. Note the following examples:

W. T. Grant
Interstate Department Stores
Stern's of New York
De Pinna of New York
Best and Company of New York
Arnold Constable of New York (founded in 1825)
Wanamakers of New York (many years ago)
Hearn's of 14th Street, New York (many years ago)
Boutique stores of the 1960s (national)
Specialty stores (constantly)

These examples are cited because retailing was once considered one of the easy ways to become an entrepreneur and make money. In today's world, fashion marketing has become a highly specialized area with intense competition. Good retailing demands constant research and reassessment of consumer characteristics, demographic and psychological. Success is maintained through vigilance; failure to reassess customers is one of the sure roads to oblivion. To mention one small example of the change in customer preferences, who would have imagined that the very strong junior department would have anything but dresses? In the 1960's dresses were a minor category in junior dress departments!

The retail sector accommodates different income levels by a

retail mix of location, merchandising policies, and service and communication.

Obviously, stores catering to the higher income levels establish themselves in "right" neighborhoods; offer high-priced merchandise in the early stages of fashion acceptance; and make available services that include personal selling. At the other end of the spectrum, stores with low-priced merchandise sell from low rental locations; have merchandise on pipe racks; offer no personal service; operate on a cash-and-carry basis; and set price levels at the lowest possible denominators.

The important point is who is your customer, what is the satisfaction sought, and at what price level?

Below are a few situations in which research affected the marketing of apparel.

When Yves St. Laurent opened his Rive Gauche shops in America, his organization was after that segment of customers with money. The stores would not offer blouses at $15 or $20, which are available in department stores.

They made demographic and psychographic studies. One of the first location choices was New York City. One of the choices after that, based on income figures, could have been Boston, which is part of the SMSA of Boston-Lowell-Brockton-New Hampshire, one of the leading SMSAs in the United States, but the decision was negative. Why? It was decided that psychographically the price levels of the merchandise were repugnant to Bostonians. Result? A decision to bypass the city.

One of the best research examples concerns a store currently enjoying a reputation for being "with it"—Bloomingdale's of New York. Just a few years ago, there were stories in the news about the store entertaining the Queen of England on her visit to America; and the opening of two stores in the Washington, D.C., area with fanfare and tremendous national publicity.

Did all this happen by accident? No. Sometime before World War II, Federated Department Stores, Inc., the owner, made an in-depth survey that showed that the then popular-to-medium-priced store was advantageously located in an area of flux. The East River and environs were being rebuilt and developing a population of high income and specific taste levels that one could call the "forward generation." Recognizing these factors, the retail mix was changed and the character of the store lifted upward to satisfy the new customer mix.

This all happened in a period when other stores in the same general area of New York City were failing.

The moral is that research is needed and the marketing direc-

*Planning*

tions suggested by the findings implemented—one of these findings being income level of the segmented market.

## Summary

The uniqueness of fashion apparel marketing is without question based on the consumer's attitude about wearing clothes, and falls into the class of personal consumption. Although many would argue that the availability of choices permits the selection of essentially the same fashions at any price, clothing at different price levels has different characteristics. The ingredients of the garments, how they fit, when they are available, and sometimes their serviceability are all related to retail cost.

There can be substantive differences between the clothing worn by a person whose income is $100,000 and that of an individual who earns $10,000. The silhouette, details, colors, and sometimes even the fabric may be the same, but variations are easily discernible to an objective viewer. What makes the difference is the quality, and, of course, the frequency of purchases.

Another unique value is the fact that never in the history of the world have so many people enjoyed the right and ability to be in fashion. There are several reasons for this:

1. The ability of markets to mass produce at all prices.
2. The standard of living of most Americans—there is sufficient income to allow for approximately 10 percent of disposable income to be used for the purchase of clothing so as to be in fashion.

## 10. LOCATION

### Introduction

The "right" location is essential for the success of a retail store. Retail transactions are initiated by consumers who have the option of going to any store that offers the greatest satisfaction. In such a highly competitive environment, a retailer has to stock consumer-wanted merchandise in a consumer-convenient location. Both these conditions have to be satisfied before an owner can stimulate patronage. The only exception to convenience is when the retailer can offer something in its place—unique value, product, price, service, ambience, or some other consumer benefit—that motivates people to buy despite the inconvenience. In addition, a small store has only a limited ability to draw traffic. Yet it must try to meet competition with a restricted stock assortment, shallow stock depth, and limited price ranges.

Small store entrepreneurs therefore have to offset these negative conditions by capitalizing on a small store's advantages: They

*Strategies and Tactics in Fashion Marketing*

can stock merchandise for a narrow and clearly defined customer group. They can offer personalized service. They can establish customer relationships that support strong patronage loyalty. Perhaps most important, they have to have the right location.

Arriving at the right location involves three decisions:

1. the most favorable trading area, or community,
2. the most favorable site within the area, and
3. the rental cost compared to potential sales.

**Trading Area.** The term "location" has two meanings—a trading area and a specific site in the area. The *trading area* is the surrounding area or community from which most of a store's trade is drawn. This area has to contain enough potential customers with the appropriate characteristics of income, age, profession or job, and with the buying habits that suit the store's products. Every retailer, regardless of size, must therefore segment a market and identify a group of people to be served.

**The site.** After determining the most suitable trading area, the next step is to select a specific site within it.

**Rent.** A high-traffic location commands high rent, and a low-traffic one can be leased for a relatively low cost.

The dilemma is: Which combination of factors makes for the most appropriate place to do business within the limits of available capital, planned sales, and the cost of doing business? A careful investigation of all the aspects of location—general and specific—can lead to the most appropriate site, an extremely important decision in starting a solid business. (Another method of site selection is, of course, the purchase of a going store, a circumstance that is not within the range of this book.) Gathering adequate information takes some time, effort, and analytical ability. It also obliges you to discuss the data you accumulate, along with your conclusions, with an accountant or business advisor.

## Managerial Requirement

**Researching the Trading Area.** The most basic question is whether a trading area is capable of supporting the proposed store. The first step is therefore to assess the selected market's ability to yield sales for already established stores. This sort of research can lead to several important conclusions:

- the ability of the location to support the proposed store;
- the market share owned by established stores, their level of

## Planning

competition, and the proposed store's probable ability to meet the assessed strength of competition; and

- the estimated ability and willingness of the market to buy particular types of merchandise.

With reasonable care, you can also develop evaluations that you can apply to questions about other trading areas' current adequacy and growth potential.

Several sources and information-gathering methods enable researchers to arrive at meaningful conclusions.

**Preliminary Research—Buying Power Index.** For preliminary data, a well-stocked library should contain several sources of generalized information. *Sales Management,* a business periodical, compiles data that can be used to appraise an area's ability to support retail activities. These studies (called "Buying Power Index" and prepared annually by the editors of the publication) include three demographic and economic characteristics of areas:

1. population,
2. effective buying income, and
3. retail sales.

This information, although valuable, does not permit you to precisely evaluate narrow trading areas or strength of current and future competitors. But they can serve as the logical approach to research; you can establish a premise, obtain introductory material, and then follow through with specific data.

**The Standard Industrial Classification.** Published by the Office of Management Control, this manual contains a system of classifying most of the basic economic data of the nation. It provides a sound definitional basis for the collection of business data by government agencies. Each business activity is divided into groups and identified by code numbers. Although this information is too general for the purpose of small-store ownership research, the SIC codes are used by *County Business Patterns* and the *Dun and Bradstreet Reference Book,* both of which can supply detailed information about firms in more specific areas, about the level of competition, and about other pertinent information.

**Fairchild's Financial Manual of Retail Stores.** Published annually, this source contains data about major store ownership, financial details (sales of the past five years), record of profit, and executive personnel.

**Sheldon's Retail Directory.** This director lists department, specialty, and chain stores of a wide range of trading areas in every state.

*Strategies and Tactics in Fashion Marketing*

It also includes personnel lists that enable a reader to estimate ballpark yearly sales figures for selected stores.

**Observational Research.** More specific information involves some shoe-leather effort and "eye-ball" observation. The following are suggested methods:

1. A *walking tour* of the residential area of a selected location. Note the type of homes, cars, and atmosphere of the area. What is probable income range of the residents? Are there other clues as to which type of merchandise would meet with the greatest acceptance?
2. Speak to residents to determine their views about:
    a. the present and future population mix,
    b. current and future area growth,
    c. opinions, attitudes, and beliefs of residents, and
    d. planned community projects that have economic meaning.
3. Investigate the level of retail saturation or undersaturation. To determine these important factors, ask questions about:
    a. the number of stores that sell similar lines of merchandise,
    b. the number of empty stores,
    c. previous and current retail employment rates,
    d. sales per square foot of selling area of stores (Chamber of Commerce, local trade organization, local real estate organization), and
    e. general information from the personnel of the local bank and local small business association.
4. Take a head count of customers passing and entering stores. This sampling should be done over an extended period. Here are a couple of suggestions:
    a. Counts should be taken during store-open hours on six consecutive days, excluding holidays and sale event days, when traffic is abnormally high.
    b. Observe traffic of specific departments that stock the same or similar merchandise of the proposed store.
5. Examine newspaper advertisements to evaluate the type of goods featured by retailers for fashion prestige and promotional purposes. This technique can give evidence of:
    a. the strengths and weaknesses of competition,
    b. merchandising opportunities, and
    c. customer attitudes about fashion merchandise.
6. Take the license plate numbers of cars in the parking areas. Although time-consuming, of course, this method identifies customer characteristics of: where they live, income range, and mobility. (This information must be obtained from a local license bureau.)

## Principles or Practices

Since the beginning of recorded history, retailers have tended to cluster together in groups of competing and/or complementary stores. Clustering is a way to serve customers' needs best by minimiz-

*Planning*

ing purchase effort. So wherever people reside or frequent in sufficient numbers, a retail market of stores develop in a cluster.

Following World War II, the mass exodus to suburbia caused retailers to respond to the needs of newly developed communities. Department stores extended their operations by opening branch stores. Discount and mass operations appeared with unparalled rapidity. Chains extended their number of units, many specialty shops becoming chains. Every retailer to some degree was affected by unprecedented and continued population movement. Over the years, the rapid shift of markets resulted in an environment in which retail business is now conducted in virtually every trading area within and outside of municipal boundary lines. In fact, many geographic boundary lines between city and suburbia have been blurred and flow into each other.

These events results in the formation of four major types of retail cluster institutions:

1. the central business district,
2. the regional shopping center,
3. the community shopping center, and
4. the neighborhood shopping center.

**Location Characteristics**—Wherever most Americans live and/or frequent, retail sites and their characteristics fall into a number of commonly encountered classes, which should be weighed as part of your investigation of a particular site:

**Downtown Core**—located in a central business area; high rental zone; limited parking facilities; pedestrian traffic; big store competition.

**Downtown Frame**—outer part of the urban environment; relatively low rental; best suited for dealers in autos, lumber, hardware, and building materials.

**Strip Development** (Radial Site)—usually situated along major traffic areas connecting central business districts and residential areas; best suited for convenience goods; prone to "deterioration" due to a lack of long-range planning.

**Interceptor Ring**—outer loop of an urban area, frequently at the outer section of two or more principal thoroughfares; usually service stations and thirty or forty stores; possibly an important site due to its nearness to residential section and traffic.

**Peripheral Site**—outreach of city; adjacent to highway or access road; high traffic; usually beyond zone of municipal taxes; "unplanned" buildings; generally well suited for a mass merchandising operation.

**Isolated Location**—lack of other retail stores; low rental; most appropriate for local convenience store or discount operation.

**External Site**—along traffic artery between communities—depends on highway traffic; low rental; sometimes as part of cluster of stores.

**Mall and Shopping Center**—clusters of stores that can be included in the forementioned sites; most often dominated by two or more major outlets, large branch units of a department store or national chain operation; high customer traffic; planned parking area; high rental; in-premise competition; mall enclosed and arranged so that ambience encourages leisurely shopping.

**Site Criteria.** After considering a trading area's importance and the type, there are the final criteria for selection of the specific site.

**Number and Quality of Customers.** The first qualitative aspect is the number and quality of potential customers who pass the site. High traffic in itself does not necessarily mean many potential customers. Traffic flow can even have a negative effect on a site where people are in a hurry or have no place to park a car. As an example, thousands of people pass by stores in major railroad terminals, but how many are inclined to buy a dress or suit in such an environment?

An additional consideration is that some sites have an uneven traffic flow. A store operated in an office building in a business area would be closed on Saturdays and have no business during the evenings. Its best traffic would be during the hours from noon to 2 p.m., with additional consumer interest after 5 p.m.

Although these examples involve high-traffic sites, for certain products the value of a traffic count must be weighed against consumer motivational factors: Is it the right time and the right place to purchase given products?

A retail axiom is that competition attracts greater traffic—provided, naturally, that the competition is equal and fair. People are prone to shop in sites that have several stores carrying similar lines so they can make comparisons and decide on value. And indeed, shopping centers often have tenants who are in direct competition with each other, but the total of retail business generated is far greater for each then if they did not coexist.

*Planning*

Conversely, what is undesirable is a neighboring store that is incompatible with your manner of doing business, your merchandise, or any other condition that adversely effects business. For example, a specialty shop that sells moderate to better merchandise would be ill-positioned next to a butcher shop. A bridal shop abutted by a pizza parlor would not be conducive to better business. And, to use an extreme, what apparel store would want a graveyard for cars as a next-door neighbor? On the other hand, price-maintaining apparel store owners would prefer neighboring stores that carry shoes, children's wear, or any other merchandise that attracts the type of customer they serve. Good interrelationships among neighboring stores, depend to a great degree on product compatability, on the manner in which business is conducted, and on the customer groups for whom merchandise is intended.

As a consumer convenience, give serious thought to parking facilities. In some main street suburban areas, stores have been forced out of business due to the lack of parking space. In the absence of space convenient for potential customers, what appears to be a highly desirable site could be a poor risk. How much space is required is relative to a particular site, to the time and frequency of shopping hours, and to the manner in which business is conducted—all rather broad guidelines. Although there are no precise guidelines, a rule of thumb is that a specialty shop requires four to five spaces per 1,000 square feet of store space.

**Lease Commitment Terms.** Once a site is selected, the final arrangement is the signing of a lease for a given term. (It goes without saying that a lease should not be signed until it has been examined and explained by an attorney.) The most common forms of leases are:

1. *Flat amount for a year*—a fixed amount to be paid each month.
2. A *straight percentage*—stipulates that a percentage of sales or profit shall be paid.
3. A *percentage with a guaranteed minimum*—the tenant pays on the same basis as a percentage lease except that the landlord is guaranteed a minimum sum regardless of sales or profit.

The limit of affordable rent for a specialty shop is 9 percent of net sales. So certain desired sites may be beyond your proposed store's capacity to operate successfully. In the final analysis, picking the most desirable site must be done only after comparing the cost of rent with potential net sales. If the "numbers" necessitate the selection of an "80 percent" location, for example, you must realize the necessity to create a store that has the value of uniqueness for potential customers, such as:

*Strategies and Tactics in Fashion Marketing*

- unusual personal service,
- merchandise that targets consumer needs,
- the arrangement of merchandise that pleases consumers, including dramatic window displays,
- fashion shows with prophetic merchandise, or
- pleasant store ambience.

Location is a primary and critical concern. First you must identify your consumer group target and trading area, as well as determine that they satisfy each other. Once the trading area requirement is satisfied, you can decide on a particular site. But your decisions should be based on the most thorough research efforts—the weighing of all plus and minus factors.

# SECTION THREE

# Selling: Sales Promotion

HOW MUCH IS SOLD in units and dollars, at what speed to minimize investment, at what cost, are critical marketing concerns. The bottom line of a profit and loss statement is net profit, but the first line is sales.

The development of an effective communication mix is one of the most important requirements of marketing success. Even though the definition of sales promotion is hazy, it is generally agreed that it is the coordination of all seller-initiated efforts to set up channels of information and persuasion to facilitate the sale of a good or service. This encompassing range of activities requires planning, cost, and purpose.

The five units of this section are related to selling efforts or manufacturer and retailer opportunities.

Article 14, "Non-Store Retailing: A New Apparel Opportunity," is a subject that will assuredly have a profound effect on future retailing and could have been included in Section Four. However, it concerns a current method of selling and, therefore, is related to the other articles of this section.

Within the five units of this section, there is coverage of the comprehensive meaning of sales promotion, their activities and guidelines for their applications for both manufacturers and retailers (with improvisations, for textile producers).

## 11. OPPORTUNITIES THROUGH SALES PROMOTION

The basic consideration of sales promotion planning is a marketing objective. Like most other businesses, fashion apparel firms are concerned with the general marketing goals of product distribution, customer loyalty and a national brand position, if it is within the constraints of available resources. However, the unique characteristics of the industry and the product necessitate the utilization of particular strategies and tactics, which vary with firms depending upon organization size, volume, distribution and product characteristics.

A plan, therefore, must respond to corporate objectives, the selection of those activities that are most likely to succeed and are within the restraints of a budget.

In discussing sales promotion, it is necessary to define a rather loosely used term, which is most often referred to as advertising. Actually, it is "any means that influences the purchase of a product or an idea." It follows, therefore, that the range of activities is wide, and requires a plan to select the ones that are most appropriately related to the aforementioned conditions.

Sales promotion activities are classified into two types: *personal* and *nonpersonal,* of which the former is used most widely. As a matter of record, apparel producers as a group spend less than 1 percent of net sales for *advertising*. However, if a marketing objective is to seek a national brand position, obviously the cost must exceed this low rate, and advertisements must be run with required frequency in national media.

Our focus is on the average or small size company with a limited budget, which necessitates careful planning and selection of goals and media.

The most common and effective promotional availability is a *sales force*, which engages in the personal activity of sales promotion. Therefore, when a company develops a line, changes its product, or simply wants to increase sales, the most productive and responsive means is readily available.

Through the means of a clearly developed message that a staff can comprehend and decode, a firm has a marketing "tool" that has the greatest influence in solving these needs. Personal selling is costly, it is true, but it is most productive and should be the core activity of sales promotions, the major advantages of which are:

- Qualitative control of distribution
- Immediacy and measurability of selling efforts
- Feedback and market intelligence
- Communications tailored to specific retail needs
- Explanation in response to customer objections.

In comparing the essential values of personal selling and mass advertising, it can be seen why the vast majority of firms depend upon a road staff, and why it is necessary to arm it with sufficient and powerful promotional information. But personal selling hardly satisfies the market objectives of fashion producers.

## Selling: Sales Promotion

Despite budget limitations there must be the addition of at least some nonpersonal activities. Therefore, media and related activities will be discussed from the viewpoint of practicality and reduced to those items within the budgets of most companies.

The following are the suggested media that merit most serious consideration:

- Fashion magazines
- Trade publications
- Direct mail
- Publicity
- Directories
- Catalogues
- Point-of-purchase displays (including hangtags and merchandise box wraps)
- Co-operative advertising
- Fashion shows (including trunk showings)
- Editorial credits.

For over 100 years, American fashion magazines have been carrying company messages to ultimate consumers, and, in some degree, influencing retailers. The most noteworthy advertiser advantages are the relatively minor cost to reach an audience on a national scale and a readership that far exceeds distributed copies.

However, the "red herring" is that the value of advertising is proportionate to frequency and the need to feature generic styling. These conditions are warranted when the main objective, as noted, is to obtain a brand position. As a counterbalancing advantage, however, ads can be merchandised effectively, re-prints obtained and used as direct mailers to retailers. A specific promotion for a limited period can be considered as a way to claim national product importance.

In addition, sales personnel are usually more than anxious to carry evidence of "published" styles in their "bag of tricks" and use them as part of sales presentation. Without going into depth about magazine publisher inducements—such as inclusion in fashion shows, special hangtags, and advertisers' listings—the fact remains that limited budgets inhibit the use of a medium that does not assure a selling return and has questionable merit for single or infrequent ads.

Direct mail can be a powerful promotional force, particularly if mailing pieces are prepared by the manufacturer and then sold at a minimal cost to cooperating retailers who in turn send them to their customer list. This strategy has the advantages of early order receipt from participating retailers, wide distribution of merchandise, and strong opportunity for reorders. The method has an inherent promotable factor—the measurement of sales return as compared with sales promotion cost.

The direct mailing piece prepared and sent by the manufacturer to retailers to influence wholesale selling has some, but limited, return value. Buyers purchase infrequently from mailing pieces. They receive a steady stream of market information from their resident buying offices, including bulletins about particular manufacturers and specific styles. Parenthetically, a manufacturer's use of resident buying office bulletins is an effective and low-cost sales promotion activity. It is another type of promotion that is sales measurable and widely used.

*Publicity*, an unsponsored and non-paid message, is a highly desired form of sales promotion since it reflects an objective point of view of a publication. Much publicity is firm-inspired and submitted to a suitable medium. Because most firms do not have a public relations employee, the likelihood of continued and/or planned "free advertising" is remote. However, a related activity, an editorial credit, which features a firms' garments and retail stores where they can be purchased by ultimate consumers, is within the sales promotion range of many.

*Directories* serve the useful purpose of identifying the specialties of manufacturers and their locations. A promotional budget should include an allotment, which is really an insignificant cost, for publications such as retailer market guides and building directories. Out-of-town buyers, particularly, use these publications, and even though there is no yardstick that measures their sales return, they are a necessary sales promotion expenditure.

*Catalogues* and *mailing pieces* are related and most effective when they are part of retail store promotional efforts. The advantages of a store catalogue feature are essentially the same as a store mailing piece. However, the average cost of participation in retail catalogues is high. If participation is a selected promotional activity, it is well to pick particular stores in separate trading areas of major importance, and concentrate on the catalogues distributed during the period(s) when the merchandise has greatest consumer appeal (i.e., Christmas, Easter, fall opening).

As a competitive practice, store merchandisers study the catalogue-featured garments of other stores. Catalogues, therefore, can be considered as a sales promotion activity to attract buyers within given trading areas. Interestingly, in a business of insecurity in which "follow-the-leader" is an indigenous practice, a major store catalogue has a strong impact on other retailers. "Knocking-off" is an all pervasive practice by both manufacturers and retailers.

## Hangtags and Point of Purchase Displays

*Point-of-purchase displays* and *hangtags* are given minor importance too often in planning a sales promotion campaign. It is true that manufacturer built displays cannot be used by many stores due to policies about size and "decoration" that detract from established decor. However, displays, if constructed artfully and judiciously distributed, can be an important method of accelerating sales, particularly of classic garments, that are available in a wide range of colors.

An important resource of men's shirts has signal success with sales counter racks that feature up to 20 different shades. This strategy gives merchandise prominence to a degree that it dominates many men's shirt departments, a highly desired advantage. The fallacy is that the racks are often used for competitors' goods, and therefore require policing.

Hangtages are a potential source of customer annoyance. It is well for a manufacturer to carefully plan and restrict hangtags to customer-understood essentials. Hangtags are a message from producer to user and should be designed to generate consumer attention and understanding with limited effort.

In a day when self-service is pervasive—even in retail stores that purport to avail personal service—a manufacturer must use every possible means to attract customer attention. Box wraps that are often stocked on open retail shelves can be attractive attention-getters with considerable sales promotion value. Quality boxes and wraps should be considered an important phase of sales promotion. The advantage far outweighs the cost.

*Co-operative advertising* is, in reality, a reduction in the garment's wholesale cost that affects a manufacturer's net markup—unless there is a three-party arrangement under which expenditures are assumed by, for example, a textile or fiber supplier. As a matter of law (the Robinson-Patman Act), retailers must be offered equal terms on a proportionate basis—as a percentage of net delivered goods. Because advertising affords manufacturer assurance of initial order placement and the probability of reorders, related, of course, to consumer acceptance, co-operative advertising is a subject that should be weighed carefully as an integral part of promotional plans.

*Fashion shows* are really not nonpersonal. As a sales promotion activity they can be a strong influence in accelerating sales to both retail and ultimate consumers. Shows that are held in the market for retailers can be a problem because market week time must be husbanded by buyers, and time for fashion shows is concentrated on those of the most important manufacturers.

Firms seeking market status are well advised to obtain profes-

## Strategies and Tactics in Fashion Marketing

sional services to attract a desired buyer audience. The easiest fashion show is the manufacturer sponsored in-store event. This promotional ploy can solidify relations with retailers and create special orders from customers—the type that eliminates store inventory and reduces selling cost. To hold the cost to a minimum, a manufacturer can use a store's auditorium, store customers as models, and prepare such events with an employee fashion director.

Another alternative is a *trunk showing,* a pre-season (or current season) presentation of an entire line in a store's appropriate department. In this instance, the territory salesperson can present the merchandise; models, again, can be customers, and expenses can be borne by the firm, salesperson, or shared. A strategically planned series of trunk shows can be held at little cost and result in a strong sales stimulant.

A limited budget demands analysis of each component of a sales promotion plan and its probable influence and coordination with the total strategy to reach the intended marketing objective. As noted, this discussion does not include the options of service magazines, T.V., and radio that are open to the larger firms with extended budgets.

## 12. SALES PROMOTION

### Definition

Sales promotion is the third "P" of merchandising; it follows planning and purchasing, and should lead to the last "P"—profit. Profit can only be realized as a result of selling, therefore all retailers are deeply concerned with the sales promotion effort.

The term, sales promotion, has been defined in numerous ways, but for our purpose, it is any means that influences the purchase of fashion apparel. From the buyer's point of view, the two major objectives are:

1. Customer patronage for the department
2. Acceleration of sales

Naturally, a store requires the buyer to plan for and participate in events that have wider objectives: store patronage motives, institutional values, and prestige.

What strategies and tactics are used are dependent upon what customer group is sought. Lord and Taylor and Korvette's, for example, employ different techniques to influence their selected audiences.

## Fashion Promotion Media (including personal selling)

The following means of promotion are used to influence customer buying decisions.

**Personal Selling.** Personal selling ranges from full- to no-service. The level of availability is dependent upon the nature of the retail operation. Unfortunately, even where it is available, the quality is often less than adequate. Since it is the highest cost of doing business outside of the cost of the merchandise, it is reasonable to assume that it will deteriorate even further. Good salesmanship can avail all or any combination of the following advantages:

1. Highlighting garment features
2. Motivating customers to purchase apparel
3. Enhancing patronage motives for the department
4. Solving customers' "problems"
5. Suggesting additional merchandise
6. Obtaining customer feedback

**Newspapers.** Newspapers, as a medium, receive the lion share of a fashion department's promotional budgets because:

1. They reach 90 percent of all U.S. families with an appeal to each member of the family.
2. The cost per reader is less costly than any other means.
3. They have the longest span of potential customer interest. The consumer reads newspapers at his leisure which makes for the greatest concentration and impact.
4. The response to advertisements is relatively fast and measurable.

**Magazines, Independent Shopping Publications, Radio, Television.** Magazines, independent shopping publications, radio, and television are all used in a minor way, with greatest concentration on institutional values. It should be mentioned that television can be the next best form of advertising to personal selling. It has color, motion, sound, and the human voice (spoken by a well-trained, attractive person). Television has all the elements for fashion selling, except the cost.

**Direct Mail.** Direct mail is a widespread form of fashion merchandise promotion, most often in the form of statement enclosures and catalogues. Newspaper ads that feature mail and telephone, although not considered direct mail, are strongly related to it and represent a well-used, successful means to volume selling by many stores.

Direct mail and mail and telephone advertising are of deep concern to the buyer because:

1. They represent a big business that continues to grow.
2. Increased customer leisure time, oddly, has an influence in establishing them as a modern way of shopping.
3. Lack of stores' quality personal service has further influenced impersonal shopping habits.
4. Customer recognition that impersonal selling methods require high standards of quality and garment specifications. (Organizations that use mail and other impersonal methods.)
5. They afford the retailer the ability to reach particular groups of people (by income, ethnic value, charge customers, etc.).

**Fashion Shows.** Fashion shows are one of the most exciting methods of influencing customers to purchase fashion goods. Practically everyone enjoys the drama and excitement of a show of new fashions that include: attractive models, music, and a festive atmosphere. Fashion shows also show fashion authority, no small attribute to attract customers.

A small store is at no disadvantage and can stage periodic events to prove its importance in the fashion world of its community.

Larger stores offer presentations in auditoriums and selling departments, frequently department showings in the form of "trunk" shows featuring merchandise of the forward season, sometimes with a famous designer present.

**Window Displays.** Window displays can be likened to the apparel one wears, they are a reflection of attitudes. Although the buyer does not control when merchandise can be featured in windows and in trafficked areas, what can be displayed on the floor is largely in the hands of the buyer. Floor displays are opportunities to expose merchandise to traffic and thereby influence customers. Wherever possible, merchandise used in other forms of promotion should be featured in the windows for added impetus and customer convenience (where to find it in the store).

It is interesting to note that many apparel chain stores in shopping centers do a minimum or no newspaper advertising, depending wholly on location and traffic to obtain a local market share of fashion business. In these instances, window displays are most carefully planned and evaluated.

**Floor Displays.** Of equal importance, perhaps greater for the

## Selling: Sales Promotion

buyer, is the floor display of a fashion department. This is where the store attitude, department point of view, and fashion knowledge are revealed to the customer. A smart buyer seeks, accepts, and uses the aid of all staff personnel to make the department "smart" looking and the merchandise salable. The fashion coordinator and display people are staff personnel who are available for help or in charge of the activity.

## Responsibility for Sales Promotion

Since promotion is one of the major components of the retail mix (and merchandising activities), management sets rules concerning:

1. Goals
2. Format (logo, artwork, layout, etc.)
3. Budget (percent to net sales)
4. Media
5. Responsibility
6. Calendar of events

In a larger store, sales promotion is the responsibility of the Sales Promotion Department (sometimes called the Advertising Department), with a separate subdivision which concentrates on activities involving catalogues and direct mailing pieces.

**The Buyer's Role.** Obviously, merchandise required to support promotional events is purchased by the buyer.

The event starts with a store plan drawn up by the general merchandise manager who then allocates budgets to the various divisions. The divisional merchandise manager then plans a calendar of events with each buyer which includes:

1. Date
2. Space
3. Purpose

The discussion additionally includes the following merchandising factors with strong buyer input:

1. The buyer's selection of resources
2. The merchandise
3. Volume potential
4. Reorder probabilities
5. Cutoff date of selling
6. Markup

7. Retail value
8. Unit requirements
9. Timing

## The Promotional Purchase

The first step by the buyer is a plan to purchase merchandise against the available open-to-buy with the realization that:

1. The delivery must be made in advance of the promotion date.
2. The commitment will be against the open-to-buy for the month in which delivery is made (as stated above).
3. The required budget for the event was provided for in the Merchandise Plan.

The second step is to visit the selected resources, or seek resources suitable for the purpose.

These are some of the conditions that will have to be satisifed:

1. The appropriateness of the merchandise such as style, quality, price, color.
2. Resource relationship
    A. Key, or preferred, resources are most desirable since customer acceptance of the merchandise is already known.
    B. Delivery dependability.
3. Reorder possibilities—backup merchandise to be held by the manufacturer. In catalogue merchandising, this is a critical need. Errors of stock omission are serious miscalculations.

After all these conditions have been met, the buyer places the commitment (the order).

The final step is the follow-up. A vigilance to ensure timely delivery well in advance of the date of promotion. Non-delivery is considered a calamity for which management accepts no excuse.

## The Mechanics of the Promotion

As discussed, every large organization has a Sales Promotion or Advertising Department which is responsible for:

1. The purchase of space (catalogue or direct mail requirements)
2. Production of the promotion
    A. Copy
    B. Layout
    C. Artwork

The buyer furnishes merchandise and information about it so that the specialists in the Promotion Department can develop the advertisement.

Once the work is finished, it is submitted to the buyer in proof form so that the buyer can verify all the details and suitability.

*Selling: Sales Promotion*

# A Buyer Check List for Sales Promotion Purchases

1. Merchandise and resources should typify the store's image.
2. Promotional values should be realistic and honest. The Better Business Bureau has standards for: "regularly," "usually," "formerly," etc. Customers are not fooled by sharp practices.
3. Promotions should be supported with adequate stock. Early fall catalogue responses, for example, that necessitate letters of delayed delivery are annoying to customers.
4. Caution should dictate that a rate of sale should be established before "plunging" into merchandise for volume production.
5. Specification buyers (Sears, Ward, and Penney) are experts in filling catalogue requirements because they:
   A. Research the makers.
   B. Visit production facilities.
   C. Submit specifications.
   D. Double-check samples for specifications and quality. Other buyers who do specification buying for promotional events should heed these practices.
6. A buyer should understand the purpose of an ad and act accordingly.
7. The immediate sales returns from a mail and telephone order may be deceptive. If the ad is too flattering to the merchandise the returns can be heavy.
8. Newspaper advertisements can be more effective if:
   A. Window and floor displays reinforce the featured merchandise.
   B. Sales personnel is properly advised and given reasons for the promotion.
9. Unsuccessful ads should not be repeated.
10. New resources should be avoided if possible: their merchandise is new to the department, the selling rate is unknown, and the quality level is not established.
11. Cooperative advertising money should be considered as an added feature of a purchase, not the reason for it.
12. The buyer's first loyalty is to the stock of the department. It should be studied for realistic assessment of current value and marked down, if conditions warrant, to levels that reflect current value.
13. The markdown of regular goods can be a bargain for customers and reinforce patronage motives.
14. Lower priced levels should not be promoted at the beginning of a season. This is the time for higher priced concentration. Customers will look for lower prices later.
15. Off-price promotions should not be purchased in the absence of a manufacturer's inventory showing styles, colors, sizes, and quantities.
16. Orders for promotion of this type should be detailed against a manufacturers inventory, e.g. *specific* quantities, styles, colors.
17. A warehouse visit to inspect the goods is an excellent practice.

18. Job lot buying is a dangerous practice. It is available because of someone's mistakes; the second mistake can be the buyer's.
19. Promotions are a partnership arrangement between the manufacturer and the store—the manufacturer should be made aware that the store's communication also affects his relationships with customers—the store's and his own (your competition and his channels of distribution).
20. All promotional orders should specify:
    A. The fact that the order is for a promotion.
    B. The date of delivery should be discussed in depth. If there is any current problem the buyer is flirting with later trouble.
    C. All special conditions should be written on the face of the order as a confirmation of agreed terms. Conditions written on a later received confirmation order form may go unheeded.

## Conclusion

Sales promotion is a major part of the retail marketing effort and continued strong selling results depend on effective merchandising activities. The sales promotion effort must be honest, consistent, and representative of what the store is about. Every store, naturally, has a policy of what its promotional activities include and what results are expected.

A critical standard of measurement of buyer efficiency is the selling record. Retail profit is the result of a domino effect. Good planning leads to a well balanced stock; effective promotions of well purchased merchandise adds up to profit as planned—the name of the game.

The promotional results of every purchase event are recorded and used as the experience factor for future events. Buyers usually maintain a diary in which all merchandising and correlory information are entered:

1. Sales—volume for each day
2. Weather
3. Promotional event (all details—medium, space size, merchandise, etc.)
4. Any activity that influenced the merchandising results of that day. This is further evidence that:
    A. All planning is based on experience plus anticipation.
    B. All merchandising activities are measurable.
    C. Maximum profit is the result of well-conceived plans.

## 13. WHAT MAKES A SUCCESSFUL ROAD SALES FORCE—AND HOW TO BUILD ONE

Selling is admittedly the most important marketing activity. But apparel manufacturers as a group are guilty of insufficient planning in implementing a professionally-based road selling staff.

It can be said with justifiable reasons that most organizations are inhibited by limited life-span, size and capitalization. It can be further reasoned that the pace of product change, customer capriciousness, and the inability to produce lines of equal seasonal importance foster opportunistic decisions to obtain immediate or short term gains. One common failing is to hire sales representatives and have limited interest in treating them as important cogs of a marketing system.

Successful marketing-based organizations, especially those of size, first develop well-structured tables of organization that include the position of *marketing director,* under whom there is a sales manager who directs and controls the selling force. The assignments of authority, responsibility and sales accountability make for the best climate in which a sales executive can perform the necessary functions of: recruiting, selecting, training, allocating, motivating, compensating and evaluating sales personnel.

The average apparel firm, however, functions with a limited number of generalists, one of whom is a sales manager who often wears many "hats:" advertising manager, part-time stylist, salesman and production controller. But, despite lack of specialization, the important and challenging responsibility of managing a sales force in a market that is growing increasingly complex—competitively and technologically—there is the urgency to define and analyze the role of the road staff's importance to corporate health, and then develop a team that is motivated directed and controlled to attain management objectives.

Like every marketing activity requirement, there should be a clear definition of the role of a salesperson, territorial objectives, job specifications and job description. A *job specification* is a list of particular attributes a company seeks in sales applicants; a *job description* is the definition of duties that a representative must perform.

There are few firms, including some large ones, that have formalized job descriptions, despite the fact that a representative is entrusted with controlling a territory's volume, distribution and relations with retail stores. Not only should job descriptions be carefully prepared, but they should be revised periodically so that they take account of new market conditions. The benefits that can accrue from appropriately developed assignments are:

- Highlighted organizational objectives.
- Explicit duties.
- Use in setting performance appraisal criteria.

Recruiting and compensating road salespeople must be considered as closely related subjects. A new firm has great difficulty in employing seasoned salespeople with established clienteles. Any why should a successful traveler leave an established firm and a "guaranteed" livelihood for a newcomer?

An easy question to answer. He will not unless there is a trade-off: a guarantee of extraordinary benefits. Certainly, it is easy to fill the roster with constant travelers, those who represent lines for short periods with no signal success. This is no panacea. As a reasonable conclusion, a firm must pay (or invest) for talent, or have some provable potential strength to attract representatives who have current success. However, once a distribution system is in place, with relations established with stores, the task is simplified. With measurability of current territory potential volume, promising newcomers with area familiarity knowing store locations and buyers, either having been trained by the firm or a competitor, can be "broken-in."

Compensation sometimes becomes a debatable issue, particularly when the earned commission of a salesperson exceeds the salaries of top executives, or when drawing is in excess of a salesperson's current estimated earnings. Commissions are part of the cost of doing business and must be accounted for in the pricing of goods. However, there is another side of the issue that should be part of compensation policy (or philosophy). A firm's net worth includes good will, a value that requires the combination of proper merchandise, and gained in no small degree by the time, effort and influence of a selling staff.

Hence, the interpretation of compensation is analogous to taxes. Paying high taxes is the condition of high income; the payment of an insignificant sum, without consideration for tax shelters and other means of reduction, indicates low income. No one complains about a high tax rate until a high income is realized, an advantageous position to be in. Enlightened firms, therefore, consider high sales staff earnings favorably, a form of investment to achieve a balanced, well-maintained distribution system, which is an asset that reflects success.

## Training a Sales Staff

Once a sales staff is established, training should become a concern. The training of sales personnel in the apparel business has not received the attention it warrants for a variety of understandable reasons: limited organization size, cost, lack of sales training person-

## Selling: Sales Promotion

nel, the desire to get representatives out into the territories to produce volume, and the philosophy that "salesmen are born, not made." However, the attitude and efficiency of a sales staff often reflects management's thinking. There is genuine need for a firm to prove the merits of its product for potential customers, its concern for the well-being of its staff, the selling techniques that are likely to influence the selected market segment, and that there is sufficient trust in representatives so that they can be empowered to use discretionary terms to overcome customer resistance.

Certainly, it is unreasonable to expect relatively small-sized firms—and they are in the majority—to set up formal training programs. However, there are opportunities to develop an *esprit de corps* through a time-honored apparel manufacturer practice: the periodic sales meeting, the most practical means open to firms of all sizes.

From the outset, because the time frame of a meeting is limited, it should be structured carefully, subjects held to essentials, time periods allocated on the basis of subject importance, and the inclusion of a dialogue between management and staff. Subjects that could be considered of significance are:

- Management goals
- Marketing strategies to attain goals
- Restatement of organizational structure—personnel responsibility, including intraorganization channels of communication
- Concepts of line development
- Presentation of the line
- Selling techniques
- Role playing session
- Product potential—for management and sales staff
- Basis for establishing territorial quotas
- Feed-back—including subjects, such as: successful selling techniques used by individual representatives, line evaluation brain-storming of current problems.

There should be recognition that a sales meeting tends to develop a state of euphoria, and some attendants are prone to be carried away by an atmosphere of conviviality and become "giant killers." Too often, they return home with false notions about the importance of line elements, most frequently about new styles. Since, at the start, *they are not privy to market developments* and vulnerable to what appears to be exclusivity, not in a position to make comparisons, they are vulnerable to misjudgment. Moreover, the showing of a line on attractive models can impart a sense of importance to relatively unimportant styles.

With this in mind, a sales manager, or counterpart, should assemble the attendants into small groups and have each representative present the line from a practical point of view, just like it would be done in the field, on hangers or from hand. This is the way retail and ultimate customers will evaluate the garments in the field. In addition, there should be a *line* analysis that covers the importance of line segments, those that have been selected as being important by outside objective practitioners (cooperating buyers). In this way a firm can establish the earliest possible buyer consensus and put appropriate merchandise into production.

This strategy will give selling direction to representatives and enable them to concentrate on what probably will sell best and assure the highest percentage of delivery of merchandise ordered. By maximizing store order placement of particular styles, both management and sales staff are in the happiest circumstance—production and delivery concentration.

In an era of high travel costs, a road staff requires advances against future commissions—a drawing arrangement. A firm, therefore, has an investment that is predicated on a quota system. Good management demands current field information to evaluate the probable return (or liability) on that investment, which can be obtained from both individual order receipt and information feedback. It is well for a firm to exercise a span of control over each sales agent, the most practical of which is the use of "call", or "activity", reports. In this way, a sales manager can receive daily or weekly communications of valuable information: general selling tempo, individual efforts and sales results, comparative style importance, and merchandise selected by retailers for sales promotion events.

## Two-Way Communications

This information should be used as a valuable tool to determine probable territory yield, to exercise production control, and to establish and maintain a communication linkage between the home office and field activities. However, communication demands a two-way arrangement. If the home office treats reports lightly and does not reply to them on an individual basis, there is a strong likelihood that they will either "peter out" or take the form of non-objective automatic responses. Reports, therefore, should be responded to in a manner that indicates that the information has been digested, given credence and evaluated.

One of the nagging problems of sales management is uneven territory volume yield. The axiom is that "20 percent of a sales staff produces 80 percent of a firm's volume." It is a rarity when a sales staff consists of all "stars."

The fact is that most firms operate with "sick" territories, those that require more intense marketing effort. Sometimes circumstances call for the representation of a salesperson with a record of success who can probably pioneer or revive a territory. And in order to induce such a person to take on the task, it most likely requires the offer of terms not available to other salespeople.

This is a touchy situation. One can predict that special arrangements with one person will soon become common knowledge of the entire staff, soon enough. Hiding special treatment from a peer may require the later need to soothe the "feathers" of those who resent having to operate at lesser terms, particularly when the recipient is new to the firm. Therefore, such an arrangement should be made known to the staff as quickly as possible with an explanation. It will help to lessen or eliminate complaints or demands for similar terms.

## A Weekly Newsletter

Another communication link is a weekly newsletter to the sales force, one that is informal but contains essential information such as best-selling styles, colors, delivery information, scheduled retail ads and items of interest about representatives, success stories and social activities. But there should be a minimum of puffery or unrealistic claims, which lead to a lack of credence and the staff's attempt to out-guess sales management's motives. A poor selling style should never be touted as a "winner;" it can lead to selling mistakes, a rupture in relations between office and staff, and a communication breakdown.

An army that complains, it is said, is a most effective one. Didn't the 1978 Yankees win the World Series with a group of individualists who were characterized as *prima donnas?* But it should be recalled that management knew what it wanted, bought talented players, laid down the terms, and was consistent in its attitude. A happy and satisfied staff is one that earns high income, although it is rare for it to express satisfaction for present circumstances. It is of greatest importance for a sales force to have respect for management's marketing ability and its determination to succeed.

A great line makes for a successful sales representative, and no one can be "hot" with a "cold" line. But it takes a well-oiled selling "machine" to maximize volume and profit. Successful sales management is an important and challenging responsibility, hardly the result of coincidence or chance. It includes the planning and implementation of a calculated selling strategy and concern for the basic duties of a sales manager: effectively developing and organizing a sales staff, then motivating and evaluating it.

## 14. NON-STORE RETAILING: A NEW APPAREL OPPORTUNITY

The influences of socio-economic forces, cultural attitudes, and technology have a profound effect on the products and methods of distribution required for marketing success. During the past three decades, product innovations based on technological advances have appeared in the marketplace with unparalleled rapidity. The more recently established retail methods—branch stores, mass discounters, boutiques, and apparel discount chains—are essentially the outgrowth of demographic and psychographic changes.

That producers, retailers, bankers, and the media should have increased interest in non-store retailing as a means to profit viability in the 1980's would appear to be an anachronism. This retail method initially served a significant number of consumers in the days of frontier and widespread rural settlements, when purchase opportunities were limited. But with a current impacted population of 68 percent of Americans living on 1½ percent of the available land, and the proliferation of branch stores, shopping centers and numerous types of retailers, there would appear to be little reason for the growing importance of a non-personal method of distributing products.

Moreover, the combined factors of a mobile consumer with extended unobligated time, due to a shortened work week and time saving home appliances, should tend to encourage consumers to use more time to shop, compare values, and enjoy retail store ambience. To an extent, consumers are utilizing more time to shop, but non-store retailing has captured a considerable market share and is continuing to grow.

As a part of the premise to establish non-store retail importance, it is necessary to make adjustments in government supplied data. The basic problem is: the Standard Industrial Classification Manual, published by the Office of Management and Budget, uses obsolete terms in limiting non-store retailers to mail order houses, automatic merchandise machine operators, and direct selling establishments.

For a more precise fix on the area of our concern, we are eliminating the second category and adding: the mail order departments of conventional retailers (department and large specialty stores, etc.); non-conventional retailers, oil companies and banks; and catalog stores.

### A $60 Billion Market

Volume figures of non-store retailers are difficult to assess, but industry estimates the current annual figure as approximately $60 billion. By applying this ballpark figure against the estimated $850

## Selling: Sales Promotion

billion total retail sales of 1979, the current rate of non-personal selling is about 7 percent. This retail share can be increased dramatically with the elimination of sales of automobiles and other products that, by reason of their nature, require in-premise selling.

The following is further evidence of the growing importance of non-store retailing:

- Penney's, a newcomer to mail order selling, is doing in excess of $1 billion annually.
- Sears is now mailing in excess of 300 million catalogs a year.
- Dayton's of Minneapolis is currently budgeting 20 percent of its sales promotion effort on direct mail, an example that typifies increased conventional retailer interest in mail and telephone orders.

Catalog stores have been growing in numbers and in customer acceptance with surprising rapidity. The increased successful activities of regional operations are causing other retailers to take notice. The following selected operations have made significant regional market penetration:

Sam Solomon Company operates in North Carolina, South Carolina, Georgia and Florida. Their 480-page, 1980 catalog features over 6,600 brand name products. Their ten showrooms stock over 25,000 additional items.

L. Luria, a Florida based mail order organization, operates 100 showrooms in 22 states, with 15 to 20 additional units scheduled to open in 1980, and mails catalogs with 350 pages of merchandise description.

Service Merchandise serves customers in 22 states. Their 1979/80 catalog has 497 pages featuring essentially branded merchandise and stresses customer opportunity to obtain "full service," as indicated by the following that is part of the "how to order" section of the catalog.

Best Products, a Virginia Corporation, has showrooms in Florida, New Jersey, Ohio, Pennsylvania, California, Maryland, Michigan, North Carolina, Texas, and Florida. Their 480-page 1980 catalog features the logo "Our showrooms have put us on the map."

An advertisement in the current Best Products catalog is a classic example of the concept expressed by Professor M. P. McNair in his hypothesis, the "Wheel of Retailing." He theorized that new forms of retail institutions generally obtain a foothold on the retail scene by emphasizing *price appeal made possible by low operating costs.* In due course they upgrade their facilities and services, which necessitates added investment and higher operating costs. In time they emerge as higher priced retailers and vulnerable to newcomers with innovative methods of doing business.

It is interesting to note, therefore, that the mass discounters who were newcomers in the 1950's, as exemplified by Korvette's, are being challenged by a type of catalog store that is operated on the basis of minimal retail "trappings;" low inventory level, less than normal markup, cash terms, etc.

Non-conventional retailers, such as oil companies and financial companies (e.g., Citibank and American Express), have entered the mail order business with both feet, offering a range of merchandise that includes cameras, T.V. sets and some apparel. Their success can be attributed partially to attractive advertising and immediate consumer credit availability. These newcomers to retailing, obviously, have reasoned that non-store retailing is a fertile ground for business expansion. This well may be a retail sector that could offer a serious challenge to conventional retailers in the 1980's.

## The Role of TV

It is well within the realm of possibility that two available technological developments, telecommunication and the computer, could be the foundation for shopping at home as the dominant method of product distribution in the 1980's for many items of impulse, convenience, and specialty goods. But the reality is that television, up to now, has had greatest importance for the promotion of national brands, and at an extremely high cost.

It still remains for the media and product purveyors to learn how to prepare and air advertising messages at costs consistent with the volume potential of local or regional markets. Therefore, although the probable retail response to technological advances is an intriguing subject, this discussion concerns immediate opportunities —the use of mail and telephone, and catalog stores.

The business literature of 1979 included two studies that focused on non-store retailing growth. The proceedings of a conference presented by the Institute of Retail Management (New York University), held on January 12, 1979, is the source for the following excerpts:

"Experts see the possibility of explosive growth of non-store retailing."

"The distribution of specialty catalogs apparently has increased astronomically in recent years."

"The consumer is finding that most shopping is no longer a challenge, but instead is a chore which necessitates the neglect of more interesting activities."

On December 6, 1979, *Women's Wear Daily* featured a section, "The Consumer Speaks." The following are findings of a study prepared by Audrey S. Balchen, director of Fairchild Publications' research department:

*Shopping by mail:* In an effort to counteract traffic and sales declines due to energy-related problems, particularly in shopping center and mall operations, retailers can be expected to step up promotional efforts to attract direct mail as well as telephone orders.

An overall 61 percent of women responding in the study reported they buy apparel for themselves by mail—the share ranging from a low of 53 percent of women 18 to 24 years of age to a high of 67 percent of women 35 to 49. Younger mail-order customers tend to order mostly from catalogs issued by the stores. Mail-order house catalogs are relied on by older women to a greater extent than noted among the younger group, particularly among women 50 and over.

Women who have big budgets for their clothes are relatively more responsive to store ads than are other women—13 percent of those spending upward of $800 who ever buy did so mostly as a result of an ad compared with 7 percent of the women with smaller budgets.

Based on usual buying practices as of March 1979, women are more inclined to buy ready-to-wear by mail than intimate apparel or hosiery. Better than one out of five respondents often order outerwear items by mail, compared with 15 percent on innerwear, 10 percent on hosiery. About one out of three women (32 percent) occasionally order outerwear by mail; 28 percent intimate apparel; 17 percent hosiery.

## Expanded Opportunities

All indications point to the expansion of non-store retailing opportunities in the 1980's, for the following reasons:

- the continuation of the energy shortage;
- the number of working women—soon to approximate 50 percent of the work force—who will seek shopping means of greatest convenience;
- the further reduction of the work-week (four days in the 1980's?) will tend to expand consumer involvement in sports, hobbies, and other interests at the expense of store shopping time;
- smaller family size should influence a reduction in both shopping frequency and the need to use personal methods to obtain goods;
- consumer recognition that non-store retailers concentrate on product standardization and quality control, which are frequently underemphasized by conventional retailers;
- shopping in crowded stores and malls is not necessarily enjoyable;
- many consumers trust the professionalism and integrity of well-identified non-store retailers to offer in-trend, competitively priced merchandise.

These points, for the most part, relate to retailers that have had greatest success with non-apparel products. Sears, Ward's, and Penney's do considerable mail order apparel business, and apparel catalog specialists such as New Process and L.L. Bean have found their niche.

It is safe to say that increased interest in non-store retailing is well-founded and that the 1980's will see intensified efforts by different types of retailers—established and new—to attain non-store importance in their segmented markets. In this environment, there will be recognition by producers and retailers that apparel is a merchandise classification most suitable for non-personal selling, and that volume rewards could reach huge proportions.

The apparel producer who responds to this marketing opportunity will be faced with two alternatives. The most obvious strategy will be to seek and cultivate existing channels of distribution—conventional retailers who have successful non-store selling experience and catalog specialists. This manufacturer/retailer relationship will be tantamount to doing business as usual—on a specification basis—with arranged conditions of time of order placement, large order size, reorder timing, and garment specifications.

Retailers who do private branding will be comfortable with this type of merchandising, and manufacturers who are currently used as "contractors" in such marketing strategy will find little newness in approach, except in the number and types of organizations as potential customers.

## "Go It Alone"

The other alternative could be "to go it alone" and become the direct source of product availability for the ultimate consumer. Using this approach, if the manufacturer elects to maintain two systems of distribution, to retailers and ultimate customers, there will be a need for two separate operations, with two different labels, in order to avoid setting up in-house competition for retail customers—a practice stores will not tolerate.

In taking this route, the producer can use the marketing technique of obtaining qualified potential customer lists, groups segmented by demographic factors of age, income, profession, and other significant characteristics. This direct marketing concept could have important implications for style development and appropriate price levels to target the wants of particular market segments.

The negative factors of "going direct" are the requirements of professional knowledge and know-how to implement a direct sales plan; the need to build a staff to handle the delivery of one-piece orders; and the maintenance of an inventory level to fill orders on time and avoid stock omissions, a serious miscalculation in direct selling. In a sense, selling direct and being the mentor of what con-

*Selling: Sales Promotion*

sumers want, eliminating the retail middle-man, and consequently increasing margins could be fascinating conditions for apparel producer consideration.

Traditional retailers use the non-store retailing method with varying degrees of importance. But, sales promotion activities, with certainty, will be intensified to increase mail and telephone orders through daily newspaper advertisements and seasonal catalogs. What remains to be seen is whether or not the strategies will become widened and more sophisticated.

## Mail Order Divisions

By taking a leaf out of the book of large scale mail order houses, a department store, for example, could create a mail order division to do specification buying for catalogs. This strategy would entail product development, large size orders, quality control personnel, and appropriate planning. As an added element, catalog stores could be established, an idea that may sound far-fetched in view of the historical pattern of department stores following their consumers to suburbia with branch stores. However, new conditions, double digit inflation and the high cost of money, may make catalog stores a wave of the future for retailers who are bent on retail expansion.

The trend to move out of the traditional limited department store trading areas, as expressed by Bloomingdale's in establishing two Washington, D.C. branches, and Abraham & Straus branching into Paramus, N.J., were consistent with conditions of the 1970's. Obviously, many branches will be completed in the next two years that were planned in the 1970's. However, newer economic conditions, the high cost of money and the high return on cash deposits, may alter branch store expansion views.

On the other hand, catalog stores can be established with relatively minor investment and yield high returns. Department store "nationalization" is achievable through the use of catalogs and maintenance of widespread catalog stores.

In summary, non-store retailing, in due course, will take advantage of technological advances, and the methods will be more imaginative than a Jules Verne story. For the present and immediate future, there are sufficient means to employ strategies and tactics to satisfy the increasing number of consumers who can be served best by non-personal selling methods. The "players" who will exploit this improved marketing opportunity will be an interesting mix of sophisticated marketers: conventional retailers, apparel producers, banks, credit card organizations, oil companies, and current non-store retailers.

## 15. USING CO-OPERATIVE ADVERTISING MONEY

The seller's ploy of "sweetening the pot" to influence sales is as old as competition. From the beginning of modern ready-to-wear, producers of finished goods have been offering inducements to effect marketing advantages such as obtaining orders, assuring promotional quality orders, and influencing selling concentration—advertising and prominent merchandise display. In fact, "push money" was the earliest inducement, a strategy to gain placement of merchandise in store trafficked areas. This practice evolved into trade discounts with 8/10 EOM the usual terms. Which means that a bill paid by the 10th day of the month following delivery is subject to a discount of 8 percent.

Over the years, with the development of heightened competition, other forms of purchaser cost reductions were included in selling terms, among which are: F.O.B. (Free on Board) store, anticipation, warehousing allowance, markdown money, extra dating, and co-operative advertising money. What seller concessions are obtainable and to what degree hinge largely on the purchaser's importance to the seller—or the seller's market weakness. And there is hardly a buyer who has not probed or pressed for one or a combination of these advantages to increase profit. And on the other hand, there is hardly a manufacturer who has not offered additional terms.

Co-operative advertising has become "a way of life" in most industries, the cost of which is estimated as one dollar of every six spent on advertising. This marketing strategy came into the fashion industry in full force in the 1950's when chemical companies entered the apparel business with man-made fibers. Realizing the potential volume of fashion material and the related opportunity to strengthen their brand name importance, chemical companies provided considerable co-operative advertising budgets to influence spinners, weavers, finished goods producers, retailers, and ultimate consumers. As third parties to seller/buyer transactions, they were within the conditions established by the Robinson-Patman Act.

Manufacturers were in high favor of accepting chemical company largesse, particularly because the average ready-to-wear manufacturer's advertising budget has always been less than one percent of net sales. Co-operative advertising money offered opportunities for manufacturers to improve their retail distributions and also to abet their own efforts to obtain brand name indentification. Retailers were hardly averse to accepting money from outside sources to share a cost of doing business and help to promote newly developed merchandise. In due course, producers created their own co-op plans as part of a sales promotion mix.

## Selling: Sales Promotion

But what appears as a practice that should create affirmative trading relationships is not working out quite that way. Co-operative advertising is a controversial issue, with no unanimity of its value. There are advantages and disadvantages of giving and accepting "push money." Our focus is on the pros and cons as they relate to producers, and the major guidelines in establishing a co-op program.

The advantages of using a co-operative plan can start with the probability of its assuring increased sales on a short-term basis. Despite the principle that buyers should purchase merchandise, not advertising, it is not uncommon for buyers to be swayed by partially or fully paid ads. With a liberal co-op budget, a seller is fairly certain of being able to stimulate business, with large and small size stores.

Co-op ads in local newspapers strengthen a producer's brand position. In the final analysis, a brand is as strong as its distribution, insuring the ultimate consumer's ability to purchase the product with relative ease. And even though co-op ads do not allow the producer to exercise control over a newspaper's placement of a retailer's ad (or text), the prominent featuring of a manufacturer's merchandise name and logo are valuable to a marketing plan to attain brand status and other related benefits noted later.

Market penetration can be facilitated by co-op ads with retailers who have dominant trading area importance. When a leading retailer runs an ad, competitors are put on the alert with the strong possibility of "the follow-the-leader" principle coming into play. Through the industry communication network, stores in other trading areas are also informed of the ads and their results. Therefore, with a sufficient budget, arrangements can be made for ads in selected trading areas to break at approximately the same time. With strong consumer response to advertising, a producer proves the importance of his/her merchandise to a trading area's consumers, a strong base for a penetration in other markets, and the possibility of attaining a national distribution.

One of the problems of selling large-scale retailers is the necessity of pre-empting or partially displacing well-entrenched competitors. Such displacement may require impetus in the form of advertising allowances. It should be considered, of course, in the absence of third party support, the same proportionate terms must be offered to competitors in the trading area.

Since stock omissions of advertised merchandise is not a desired condition, retailers commit for promotional quantities for ad preparation. Hence a co-op ad can lead to the opportunity to prove merchandise importance in the best of circumstances—advertising force backed up by in-depth stock preparation.

Three inhibiting factors of advertising in national media are *cost, the need to repeat ads for effectiveness,* and *the inability to measure advertising return.* These limitations can be solved partially by sharing the cost of local ads with retailers. By concentrating in selected trading areas, advertising cost can be contained within a limited budget. If ads are successful, retailers may be prone to repeat them on a non-co-operative basis. And perhaps best of all, retailers' ads yield an almost immediate return in the form of initial selling and fast reorders. The promotable factor is the difference between regular and advertised selling. National media ads, it must be admitted, are not designed for short-term selling results. However, with a limited budget and the need to make every dollar yield a return, co-op advertising could conceivably suit such a plan. It should also be noted that some would dispute retailers' willingness to repeat ads that originated as co-operative efforts. As one sage remarked, "Giving co-op money is like taking dope, its habit forming."

The list of disadvantages of partnership advertising can start with the business truism that everyone prefers someone else to carry the burden of inventory. When co-op money is a major reason for a relationship, buyers often attempt to hold commitments to a minimum, with pressure on the producer to maintain fill-in or reorder stock. A hungry manufacturer is vulnerable, and a buyer recognizes an anxious seller. In many instances, a manufacturer working from a weak position may end up with an advertising share greater than the sum of the order. The net effect is a producer gamble that the merchandise will sell and that subsequent orders will offset initial "investment." The danger, however, is that holding forward stock in anticipation of future orders can be more fanciful than realistic, and as an additional factor of current business life, stock overages in an era of high money cost could play havoc with financial stability.

Subjective interests are whether co-operative participation creates closer seller/buyer relations and what happens when a program is discontinued or dries up. In the absence of continued selling success, a producer is highly vulnerable in this optimistic business.

Producers with a plan to attain national brand importance concentrate their promotional efforts in national media. When a co-op plan is put in place it is at the expense of national advertising. This factor must be weighed carefully since budgets are based on a percentage of net sales. The essential thrust must be focused on variable factors as: *the need for immediate sales return, distribution deficiencies,* and *estimated sales volume.*

A firm's critical concern is the effect of a co-op program on its sales staff. Obviously, sales personnel consider selling inducements as plus factors, particularly when third party participation influences giant-size stores to run Sunday supplement ads. In many instances, selling arrangements bypass sales representatives who are in no posi-

## Selling: Sales Promotion

tion to offer co-operative advertising deals. The following problems could develop:

- Is the salesperson paid full commission for little or no effort?
- Should the salesperson concentrate time and effort as a messenger at the expense of required effort for territory?
- What is the salesperson's relationship with the store and buyer if the budget dries up?

The term "co-operative" would suggest mutual purpose and sharing, but even a 50–50 arrangement is hardly on these terms. Stores, as a rule, do not give the producers the benefit of their lower advertising contract rate, often charging a rate comparable to a national rate.

Whether or not there is a favorable balance of advantages to implement a co-operative advertising plan depends upon a marketing matrix with objective estimates of how much time, effort and money are required to gain desired marketing goals. If a decision is made to implement a plan, the following guidelines could be followed to insure merchandise appropriateness for this purpose:

1. Is the merchandise on the upswing of consumer acceptance?
2. Does the merchandise characterize the entire line and therefore depict a desired firm image?
3. Does the merchandise have emotional value?
4. Are there merchandise features that deserve explanation?
5. Is the merchandise the most salable component(s) of the line?
6. Is the merchandise timely?

*Selling is influencing*—a stimulus to modify the behavior of the receiver. Co-operative advertising is a selling inducement to help influence others to effect a marketing gain. In modern parlance, it can be the push and shove of distribution.

# SECTION FOUR

# Trends

CURRENCY AND SENSITIVITY to developing environmental trends are conditions of organizational success. Among the fascinations of fashion marketing are the demands of responding to a wide range of domestic and international influence, and the need to develop merchandise that is apt to accommodate them.

The subjects discussed in this section are concerned with domestic and international issues. One article is presently unpublished and deals with a "foreign" business area, the automotive industry. The reason for its inclusion is that this industry's problems are not too dissimilar to those of the fashion business, and their "solutions" will have an effect on future fashion marketing.

Within the scope of the material of this section, in varying degrees of intensity, all fashion sectors' marketing activities will be influenced by the trends that are noted. In some instances, the future is now, such as the reality of the maturation of branch stores, the development of regional markets, and the import syndrome.

## 16. RETAILING AND MERCHANDISING IN THE FUTURE

### Introduction

Fashion retailing and merchandising practices reflect current environment. What and how merchandise is stocked and sold should respond to constant evolutionary changes of a dynamic society. In order to attain and maintain success, retailers and their fashion merchandisers must be up-to-date in their thinking and be able to react to change. Today's strategies may not "work" tomorrow. In fact, retail attrition can begin the day an organization first opens its doors for business and exposes its marketing strategies, when competition is able to adapt and improve the tactics employed by the initiator.

Professor M. P. McNair expressed this retail principle in his hypothesis, the "Wheel of Retailing." He theorized that new forms of retail institutions generally obtain a foothold on the retail scene by employing price appeal made possible by low operating costs. In due course they upgrade their facilities and services, which necessitates added investment and operating costs. In time they emerge as high priced retailers and vulnerable to newcomers with innovative methods of doing business.

In the not too distant future, you will be on the "firing line" with the responsibility of decision-making. The following are some important current and future trends to which you may have to address yourself.

## Consumer Trends

**The Census of 1980.** Every 10 years the Bureau of Census collects statistical data about the population that can be used, among other purposes, as planning information. Here are a few highlights of the "head count" taken in 1980 that are bound to have an impact on retailing and fashion merchandising in the remaining period of the 20th century.

51 percent of all women now work and constitute 41 percent of the country's total work force, and the numbers are increasing rapidly each year. This demographic factor causes the need to plan:

- What type of apparel is appropriate for working women?
- What is the best response to the diminished number of hours a woman has to select clothing?
- What help should be extended to today's women in planning their wardrobes?
- What is adequate stock composition, and what ambience do working women prefer to shop in?

The population in 1980 is approximately 230 million, 226 million counted plus unregistered aliens and other uncounted persons. Obviously, more people equate as an expanded market with greater volume potential.

The population movement from the Snow Belt to the Sun Belt continues at an unabated rate. During the period of 1970 to 1980, the Far West had a population increase of 40 percent, the South, 15 percent. California, Texas, and Florida considered as one unit had a 42 percent gain, with a 1980 population of 46 million!

It is apparent that retailers will pursue the migrants, established retailers will open branches and investors will construct new stores. Another result of this population growth is western and warm weather apparel will become more prevalent, shown on more lines for all seasons. Parenthetically, population losses for the same period were suffered by New York, down 3.6 percent; Pennsylvania, 0.8 percent; and Rhode Island, 2.4 percent.

In 1970, there were 20.1 million people over 65 years, or 9.8 percent of the population. This group is predicted to climb to 55 million by the year 2030, to 18.3% of the population. The implications of this increase are many, but certainly it will have considerable significance on apparel's styling, pricing, and timing.

Family income, in dollars, doubled in the decade. But living cost, measured by the consumer price index rose 98 percent, wiping out any real gain in purchasing power. If one gropes for affirmative fashion marketing value, the conclusion can be drawn that increased income nurtures consumer quality expectations, creates more potential customers for better goods. No doubt, this is a questionable conclusion.

It is necessary to identify the characteristics of a segmented population as a foundation of fashion marketing. Trends in population size, age, distribution, location of population, working women, and income have a strong impact on retailing and one of its major components, fashion merchandising; they dominate plans for the future.

**Lifestyles in the 1980's.** In addition to analyzing demographic trends, fashion marketers consider and respond to lifestyle trends. The conclusions of such research are concerned with how consumer role playing affects purchase behavior, therefore, predispositions about products, perception of products, and major purchasing influences. The following selected trends are noted for consideration.

As previously noted, women are expected to become the largest sector of the working force. Their purchase behavior should be altered by increased concern with their:

- Fashion appearance
- Desire to maintain a youthful posture
- Confidence
- Ability to deal with the external world
- Cosmopolitan attitude and knowledge
- Interest in leisure and travel
- Lack of relative concern for small price differences.

By 1990, 38 percent of all males will have attended college; by the year 2000, this figure is expected to reach 50 percent. Marketers can expect the consumer to be more sophisticated about trends, styles, and products. Additionally, lack of conformity will be accepted as a fact of life, which will result in the availability of wider merchandise choices and produce knowledge for consumers.

Increased leisure time, based on a predicted four day workweek by the late 1980's, will have a profound effect on retailing. Consumers will have interest in utilizing unencumbered time for recreation activities, which will expand retailer opportunity for selling casual styles and apparel related to athletics—active and spectator wear. Consumers will be best accommodated by retailers who concentrate merchandise according to consumer demand in specialty shops or departments; identify merchandise more clearly in advertising and display; increase outlets where customers can purchase more conveniently; and improve methods to reduce stock omissions.

The present trend to self-fulfillment should continue during the late 1980's and offer retailers the opportunity to capitalize on consumer demand for products that represent status or some form of attainment. Fashionable clothing, featuring designer names, should remain in popularity, particularly when available at moderate price levels.

Statistical (demographics) and lifestyle trends (psychographics) are coordinated to lay the groundwork for strategies that respond to current environment and the direction in which the market(s) is headed.

## Market Trends

**Imports.** The tides of imports are reaching flood level. The current yearly retail sales of foreign produced apparel approximates $30 billion, about one of every three garments sold; with the percentage of foreign made shoes over 50 percent of units sold. The probability of a more favorable trading atmosphere for American manufacturers is remote, in fact, it may become worse with market penetration by China.

The government has established grants for studies to coordinate the efforts of labor and management to build a more productive and competitive industry, and to encourage exporting.

However, until American manufacturers overcome the competitive advantage of foreign producers, American manufacturers will continue to be well-travelled.

**Retail Competition.** A fact of retailing is competition—a factor that will intensify. A recent trend that will continue is the "nationalization" of large-size organizations. These retailers are now competing in areas far removed from their home bases. As examples, among their other branch operations, Lord and Taylor has a store in Illinois and Neiman-Marcus operates in Florida. For practical purposes, many department and chain stores have become chains. And as indicated earlier in this article, large size retail operations are planning or erecting branches in the Sun Belt.

Big has become bigger and with expansion into widespread multiple unit organizations, the following will probably develop:

1. Fashion merchandisers responsibility will be narrowed to fewer categories of merchandise.
2. Merchandising will become increasingly impersonal, largely from computer print-outs (a present chain method).
3. Computers will be programmed to gather more sophisticated data for decision making, including data related to consumer attitudes.
4. Buyers will be required to attain a higher degree of professionalism and have a working knowledge of demographics and psychographics.
5. Planning and buying mistakes will tend to be big ones.
6. Regional buyers will be employed to cater to regional characteristics.
7. Specification buying should increase proportionately with size.
8. Mail and telephone business should increase in-store trading areas and other regions. Increased leisure time and customer identification of famous stores will be reasons for greater use of non-personal selling.
9. National credit systems may be offered by most stores.
10. Television fashion advertising should reach its maturity in the late 1980's. Cable T.V. and telecommunications are on the horizon which will open new vistas for fashion marketers.

At the start of the decade of the 80's, small store operators were hard hit by adverse economic conditions. By the late 1980's, it is within the realm of probability that boutiques and small stores will come into their own. Entrepreneurship has become an ambition for many who will reach the age of business maturity within the 1980–1990 era.

**Non-Store Retailing.** One of the fastest growing retail trends is non-store selling, estimated at approximately $60 billion annually. This figure was arrived at by adding non-store sales of mail order firms; conventional retailers (department and large specialty stores); non-conventional retailers; oil companies and banks; and catalog stores.

The following is evidence of its growing importance:

- J.C. Penney, a newcomer to mail order selling, is doing in excess of $1 billion annually.

*Strategies and Tactics in Fashion Marketing*

- Sears Roebuck is now mailing more than 300 million catalogs a year.
- Dayton's of Minneapolis is budgeting 20 percent of its sales promotion effort on direct mail.
- Catalog stores have been growing in numbers, size, and in customer acceptance with surprising rapidity.

The following selected catalog operations are indicative of the trend:

- Sam Solomon operates in North Carolina, South Carolina, Georgia and Florida. Their 1980 catalogue features 6,000 brand name products.
- L. Luria, a Florida based organization, operates 100 showrooms in 22 states, with 15 to 20 scheduled to open in the near future.
- Service Merchandise serves customers in 22 states. Their most recent 497-page catalog features essentially branded merchandise.
- Best Products, a Virginia corporation, has showrooms in Florida, New Jersey, Ohio, Pennsylvania, California, Maryland, Michigan, North Carolina, and Texas. Their 500-page catalog features essentially branded merchandise.

All indications point to the expansion of non-store retailing opportunities in the 1980's, the major reasons for which can be summarized as:

- The continuation of the energy shortage.
- The number of working women—soon to approximate 50 percent of the work force—who will seek shopping means of greatest convenience.
- The probable reduction of the work week (four days in the 1980's) will tend to expand consumer involvement in sports, hobbies, and other interests at the expense of store shopping time.
- Smaller family size should influence a reduction in both shopping frequency and need to use personal methods to obtain goods.
- Consumer recognition that non-store retailers concentrate on product standardization and quality control, frequently lacking in conventional retailers' practices.
- Shopping in crowded stores and malls is not necessarily enjoyable.
- Many consumers trust the professionalism and integrity of well-identified non-store retailers to offer in-trend, competitively priced merchandise.

**Regional Markets.** Since the development of modern ready-to-wear in 1920, New York has maintained the position of "Fashion

Capital of the World" for mass produced apparel. However, as part of the phenomenon that occurred following World War II, there has been a steady erosion of the city's fashion eminence due, in part, to the relocation of numerous plants to areas that offer the advantages of lower taxes, reduced fixed expenses, more convenient transportation facilities, among other manufacturer desired conditions.

In addition to the loss of production, merchandise mart construction has become a significant trend. Markets in strategically located cities are now significant competitors of New York markets. The growing importance of these newly created centers (and those created earlier) is reflected by thousands of visiting buyers, the impressive number of participating manufacturers in permanent showrooms and participation in seasonally-held shows.

Regional Mart importance is supported by:

- Chicago's Apparel Center includes 1,300,000 square feet of permanent showrooms and a 140,000 square feet Expo Center, with over 4,000 lines featured.
- Dallas houses 1,600 showrooms and more than 10,000 fashion lines.
- Los Angeles contains 2,000 showrooms, covers more than 2,250,000 square feet, shows as many lines as Dallas, with annual sales in excess of $2 billion.
- Miami International Merchandise Mart is a 22 acre complex, has 300,000 square feet and growing, with 100 percent occupancy.

These satellite markets feature:

- Adequate parking facilities;
- Wide range of merchandise for buyer comparison;
- Opportunity for buyers to exchange views in in-house restaurants;
- One stop shopping;
- Buyer convenience of evening openings (in some cases);
- Continuous social, but professionally-based seminars.

Although New York remains the premier marketplace even with expected further growth (20 percent gain is predicted by the year 2000), these new areas offer the convenience of more frequent market review and a more important "platform" for regional manufacturers.

**Technology.** Manufacturers have lagged in the utilization of technical developments. However, during the past few years, large organizations have started to add computers and automated machines to their production methods. Indeed, if the comparative advantage of cheap foreign labor is equalized, it will be accomplished by modernized plants.

The textile sector, of course, has been in the vanguard of the movement to take advantage of new technological developments. Computers are used freely in designing and producing fabrics. Man-made fibers, of course, are the products of chemistry.

Fashion merchandisers in the latter part of the 20th century will probably purchase apparel produced with the aid of computers and modern innovations. In what fabrics these styles will be made is a matter of conjecture.

## Fashion Merchandising Re-examined

The greatest deficiency in reading about fashion merchandising is the inability of a text to bring out its inherent excitement; only personal experience can accomplish the task. Career people who have been bitten by the bug often get a fever that can last the length of a career. The following is worthy of reexamination.

Fashion merchandising occurs at three levels:

1. Retail stores
2. Wholesale
3. Publications

Within these areas there is one common objective, the satisfaction of the needs of customers who are indeed "kings"—for acceptance is synonymous with fashion. But, the reason for the activity in the three sectors is the common denominator—profit—the name of the game.

How retail profit is made is a matter of marketing strategy:

- Who is to be served (segmentation)?
- Who is to be served (merchandise)?
- How it is to be served (service and communcation)?
- Where it is to be served (store location)?
- When it is to be served (timing—and relevancy to the arc of fashion)?

These marketing decisions require the employment of buyers whose experiences and abilities satisfy organizational objectives. Hence, buyer's responsibilities vary from market specialization to the total practices of the merchandising functions.

Common knowledge for all buyers, regardless of type of organization, are:

- Product knowledge
- Fashion dynamics
- Knowledge of the customer

- Buying principles, techniques and procedures
- Sources of supply
- Management goals and policies
- Mathematical relationships

Happily, the buyer's life is not a lonely one; a great deal of support can be available, and in a larger store includes the staff departments of:

- Comparison Office
- Fashion Office
- Unit Control Office
- Testing Bureau
- Research Office
- Resident Buying Office (considered a staff department)

Career opportunities are numerous and cover buying for:

- Large department stores
- Small independent stores
- Branch stores (where the branch is autonomous)
- Chain and/or Mail Order organizations
- Resident buying offices

One can easily understand that remuneration varies widely and depends upon responsibility for volume, type of organization, and merchandise handled.

Fashion merchandising takes place in almost every geographic area of the United States; the level of competition is high and it takes careful capital usage to insure balanced stocks and greatest profit returns. Methods of dollar and unit planning are used to insure proper relationships between sales and stock. Proper store assortment and depth are objectives of all fashion buyers, and the dimension of each is related to the nature of the operation. It is hoped that a point was made that there is never a condition of a model stock; perhaps it is a misnomer, a better term is reasonable equilibrium.

The reader should be aware that all business endeavors include provisions for errors. Errors of improper stock proportions can be discerned and corrected through proper use of control systems. What has not been discussed fully is the use of markdowns. It may be of surprise to learn that there is no operation that can operate without some stock reductions. In fact, there are two measurements that can cause management to raise eyebrows and put the buyer in an uncomfortable position: stock overage and lack of markdowns. When the books reflect these conditions, there is evidence of abnormal conditions. A buyer is expected to show markdowns and shortages which in themselves are not negative; it is only when the degrees of shortages and markdowns are beyond store standards, is the buyer put on the spot. So the reader should understand that stores, merchandise managers, and buyers are expected to make mistakes; infallibility is not part of life or merchandising. Being over cautious is as bad as excessive optimism.

It might be said that markdowns are an effective means of adjusting stock to external conditions: the market, the consumer, and the competition. The buyer knows the tolerances for markdowns, in fact, plans for them; but also plans to maintain a level through understanding the reasons for past markdowns.

The buyer's role in nonpersonal selling reveals the creative aspects of promotional involvement. In a large measure, the buyer must work within established boundaries, but merchandising policies still permit expression of expertise through buyers' planning and improvising required stocks in accordance with the nature and style of the segmented audience served.

The totality of merchandising efforts offers rewards consistent with efforts; one of the professions that records proof positive of achievement. A buyer operates in a society where talent is clearly visible; departmental statements do not lie.

Fashion buying is a highly paid profession. This is not to say that ex officio every buyer makes it big. As in any competitive business, there are journeymen professionals and top-rung, highly-paid experts. There must be criteria for success. The highly respected professional pays strict attention to business, knows his customers, knows his market, conceptualizes about his role, plans, controls, and promotes well. With due respect for possible criticism, we can state that these are most of the virtues needed for buying and merchandising success.

Two other factors are believed essentials for skilled buyers. One is that smidgen of intuition or feel for the business; perhaps a better way of saying it: a love for the business and a deep and abiding interest in people. This trait includes a curiosity of the role playing of the targeted group. Knowledge of demographics and psychographics are researched, considered, and part of decision making.

The one characteristic that equates with success in any endeavor is creativity, another word for imagination. Too often the term is used in conjunction with a breakthrough, a new discovery. In reality, creativity is the curiosity to solve a problem with a personal touch, a new treatment. In merchandising, it can be an imaginative way of accessorizing merchandise, unique displays, thematic promotional presentations, ways of stocking and "milking" classifications, or color coordination.

Fashion merchandising can be a rewarding career for the dedicated; the limitations are often self-imposed. Great golfers, artists, pianists, etc., are not born; they are made, not that inborn talent should be ruled out.

## Summary

What a retailer stocks is an indication of consumer needs and satisfactions. It gives evidence of consumers' income, age, other statistically summarized characteristics, their lifestyles, and products that are technically feasible. Since an inventory is a composition of anticipated consumer wants, a buyer's role is an agent for the ultimate consumer.

Merchandisers, therefore, must be conversant with the characteristics of those they serve, demographically and psychographically. In addition, merchandising professionalism requires currency of thinking, knowing wholesale and retail market trends, and the ability to respond to changes.

Competition is a constant retail fact of life. When a retailer is remiss in maintaining a consumer-satisfying stock, an appropriate retail setting for consumer convenience, or falls short of fulfilling implied or stated responsibilities, there is a competitor who is ready, willing, and able to fill the void.

As a concluding thought, perhaps repetitious, retailing is first and last for and about people.

## 17. INDUSTRY VIEWPOINT: ALTERNATIVES FOR SURVIVAL

On April 12, 1979, the United States entered into international agreements that are intended to bring a new order to the world trading system. After five years of Multilateral Trade Negotiations in Geneva, 41 nations accounting for more than 90 percent of world trade agreed on the final substantive results of the Tokyo Round of international trade talks.

The collection of pacts is the most far-reaching since world trade rules were first codified by the General Agreement on Tariffs and Trade (GATT) in 1947. As part of our government's position, the President, on November 11, 1978, said: "The Administration is determined to assist the beleaguered textile and apparel industry and is committed to its health and growth."

The Agreement is now in Congress and scheduled for debate on July 10, 1979. Despite the unhappiness and lobbying of groups that believe they are adversely affected, passage is fairly certain.

The Agreement will have salutary effects that will vary with industry. Most notably affected are those engaged in the worldwide government procurement market. Japan is presently resisting open competition for products required by its state owned industries. All producers, to some degree, will benefit by the approved United States demand to outlaw "hidden payoffs" to spur exports.

Although the Agreement has not been published, and the details are privy to the committees of industrial experts who participated in the negotiations and interested government parties, some regulations that affect apparel manufacturers are generally known (not specific schedules). Among these:

- Tariff rates will be reduced up to 60 percent (some will not be reduced), depending upon each item's sensitivity.
- The average reduction will be in the neighborhood of 15 to 20 percent.

Domestic apparel producers and labor representatives are not happy, but some admit that the Agreement could be worse, particularly if our negotiators had bowed to foreign country demands. An additional producer consideration is that the growth of quota-allowable quantities of imported goods as part of prior agreements with specific countries will continue, although the export surges caused by the accumulation of allowable increases will be eliminated or controlled.

It is apparent that the problem of foreign market penetration will not be solved by reason of international agreements. The alternatives to stem the import tide will have to be self-generated, and narrow down to the following three options:

1. The exploration and implementation of ways to export apparel (only $600 million were exported in 1978).
2. Use of available technological developments.
3. Creative international promotional efforts to popularize American designers and products.

The Department of Commerce is willing and able to lend support to export efforts. The machinery is available to put domestic producers in an improved competitive position for domestic and international markets. Our designers are becoming more important on the international scene, even in Paris.

Just as fashion itself is cyclical, the tides of the domestic apparel industry could be reversed, but it will require a bootstrap operation with full participation of the concerned parties: manufacturers, labor and government. The scene is set for producers to take the bit and coalesce all parties into a unified working group for the most critical purpose—survival.

## 18. REGIONAL MARTS' SUCCESS DRAWS INDUSTRY AWAY FROM NEW YORK

New York is considered by most as the "powerhouse" city of the world, whose "electricity" is generated by people of the most disparate backgrounds, who speak a myriad of languages, a considerable number of whom are bent on riding the "right horses" of fashion: producing and selling the right styles to the right retailers.

These activities create a frenetic pace that is heightened by seasonal visits of hordes of buyers who look forward to the excitement of a city that features the greatest variety of: ethnic and gourmet restaurants; showcases for all art forms, artists and skilled professionals, modes of transportation, and enclaves of sub-cultures. The scope and unmatched number of marketing offices of finished good makers and textile producers and its port city location are additional attributes of its acknowledged standing.

In the face of these apparent values, several questions arise about the growth of domestic fashion marketplaces.

- How can regional markets achieve success with the lack of fashion tradition and limited support sectors?
- Does a regional market's convenient location outweigh the advantages offered by New York?
- What is the basic role of a regional market—a challenge or an accommodation, particularly for manufacturers interested in national distribution?

As a basis for discussion, the term regional market (mart) for all those located outside of New York is a misnomer. Because of the rapidity of their growth, all new trading centers were characterized as regional. A more exact classification requires designation of a market into one of three types:

- A major market is national in scope, identifiable as a major base for a particular industry, or a segment of it (New York, Chicago, and Los Angeles).
- A sub-major market relies on the importance of its location to attract significant numbers of buyers and trade representatives. This type has importance to stores beyond its trading area (Dallas and Atlanta).
- A regional market serves stores within an established trading area (such as Philadelphia, Denver, Seattle, Boston and Miami).

Since the Miami International Merchandise Mart is the largest regional market in terms of trade-show frequency and number of participating manufacturers and/or representatives of the apparel and gift industries, it was selected to exemplify how and why domestic markets have been able to gain their acknowledged foothold.

Information about other markets is also included to support the dimension of their strengths for seller/buyer advantages.

We visited Miami to gain insights on its anatomy by interviewing mart representatives and visitors.

Our first contact was Cynthia Elliot, coordinator of marketing and publications. She discussed and exhibitied mart publications that were little short of overwhelming: press releases; information kit; schedules of showings; lists of participating manufacturers and their representatives; scheduled social events, fashion shows, and seminars; and a 56-page copy of "The Drummer" a monthly publication that carries news and advertisements.

Charlene Wells, who maintains a permanent office in the mart as regional representative of IM International, one of the largest international fashion forecasting firm of its kind in the world, said: "We are committed to the Miami market as an area of great potential and growth."

And as part of its cooperating activity, on January 13, 1980, IM conducted a seminar that previewed and forecasted the fashion scene and on-the-spot coverage of the spring and summer collections in Paris, Milan, London, and New York for retail buyers and exhibitors, a marketing ploy priced at $3 per ticket, including champagne.

There is no question that the mart's management has a well-conceived marketing matrix in place, and there are few tactics, if any, to be added.

The next step was an interview with the vice-president, Michael Sacks.

"Five years ago, when we took over, the apparel display space consisted of 200,000 square feet and an occupancy rate of 72 percent. Today we have 300,000 square feet and growing, and 100 percent occupancy. The total retail value of apparel and giftware is approaching $500 million," he said.

In response to "what are your plans for growth," he replied, "In the not too distant future, we will have a hotel in the complex, an international pavilion, and a widened industry base that will include electronics and interior decorating."

"One of the factors that should not be overlooked is, we are an excellent market for better priced merchandise because 15 percent of our buyer attendants are from Central and South America, many of whom represent fine stores."

Sacks feels that the Miami Mart's strengths include:

- Adequate parking facilities;
- Wide range of merchandise for buyer comparison;
- Opportunity for buyers to exchange views in in-house restaurants;

- One stop shopping;
- Buyer convenience of Monday evening openings;
- Gateway market for Caribbean, South and Central American store buyers; and
- Continuous social, but professionally-based seminars.

Bernie Liroff, executive director of the Men's and Boys' Apparel Club of Florida, said, "The salesman's plight is gasoline, and by being off the road and in the Mart, we are helping America conserve gas. Research compiled by the Bureau of Salesmen's National Associations show that sales representatives drive 30,000 to 60,000 miles per year in large vehicles. At the average cost of gasoline, representatives are spending well over $100 per week just for gasoline. He spends annually 159 nights in hotels and motels. The mart offers the opportunity to serve stores of every size in one place with greatest mutual convenience and cost."

Robert Lecort, president of the Mart, said, "We are pleased by both our ability to offer an alternative to the costly way to do business and the retailer's recognition of the time-saving advantage of being able to do business under one roof."

Mel Borenstein, director of sales for Nancy Knox, a sportswear firm, stated, "We are a small firm and cannot employ sales people to represent us exclusively. Since sales representatives carry several lines, we are at the disadvantage of receiving limited and sometimes no store buyer exposure. By exhibiting at a trade show, our merchandise is shown on equal terms with all lines, even the best known. There is no better way for us to sell goods than by participating in regional shows."

An owner of a small-sized store located in Miami expressed: "The mart serves me extremely well. Monday night openings save me time, effort and money. I don't need extra help, and I don't have to worry about who is minding the store. Also I get a needed education by being able to speak to other shopkeepers and attend fashion events."

As a "wrap-up," we returned to Sacks and posed this query: "How do you relate the mart to New York—as a competitor or an ally?"

"Listen," he replied, "there is only one New York, the greatest city in the world. Regardless of our success, we cannot compare the two cities. New York is a place that every good fashion retailer should visit to meet the executives of manufacturing firms, to review the fashion points of view of major stores, and capture the spirit of the most cosmopolitan of all cities, a necessary step to understand fashion trends. Our role is to accommodate a trading area that is wide and unique, and as such, we are one spoke of the fashion marketing wheel, with New York as the hub."

Despite his acknowledgement and retailer consensus that New York is still "kingpin," New York fashion producers and City officials have well-founded fears. Domestic markets serve realistic purposes and are here to stay. In fact, May 12–15 was set aside as Fashion Week, "the purpose of which was designed to raise the awareness of New York as being the center of the fashion industry," Charles Bonan, advertising liaison for the fashion committee that coordinated the project, noted: "New York has felt increased competition from Los Angeles, Dallas, Chicago, Atlanta, and Milan."

The following are excerpts from "Advertising Age," March 17, 1980:

"One of the biggest headaches of the fashion industry is the amount of time and money that must be devoted to trips for selling and buying merchandise.

"It is only natural that someone would devise an alternative to the traditional on-the-road approach. Hence, the emergence of the fashion mart, a central location for buyer and seller to meet.

"Economics are the key to our success," explains Cathy Eisenman, communication director of Chicago's Apparel Center. "Both our tenants and buyers profit from the arrangement. We are answering a need, so we can't help but be successful."

It takes only cursory research to establish the validity of New York's fears for the future. Moreover, reasons for current buying trips are not enhanced by present conditions, when the cost of travelling includes inflated hotel costs and limited accommodations. But the other side of the coin is, New York is still, and will remain, the core of the American fashion world. Small stores are the most numerous patrons of regional markets, but patronage is hardly confined to them. It is safe to say, regional markets have importance for stores of all sizes because of the advantages of one-stop shop, convenience, easy access to fashion trend information, and lowered buying cost.

The critical question is, to what degree will New York be affected?

In December 1978, Kurt Salmon Associates, Inc. publication, "Perspectives," noted:

"There are strong consensuses on the future of regional merchandise marts (a 20 percent gain is expected by 2000) and on the decline of both New York City and road selling as factors in apparel marketing."

## 19. THE IMPORT SYNDROME AND APPAREL MARKETING

The tides of imports are reaching flood levels. During the 1970's, the nation accumulated a balance-of-trade deficit of $81.6 billion, with an average yearly deficit of the past three years that exceeds $26 billion. In late April, the Department of Commerce announced a deficit of $3.16 billion for March, down from February's record level of $5.6 billion. This decline resulted largely from a 9.3 percent drop in the volume of imported crude oil and petroleum products, a condition that offers little solace to manufacturers beleaguered by a relentless flow of foreign products making increasing market penetration.

The Department of Commerce reported the following import increases for the period from 1969 to 1979:

| | |
|---|---|
| Petroleum | 2,089% |
| Automobiles | 341% |
| Radios, T.V.'s | 171% |
| Iron, steel | 313% |
| Coffee | 327% |
| Chemicals | 508% |

Some products, such as coffee, were affected by prices rather than quantities.

Although our exports have increased, they have been unable to keep pace with imports, hence huge trade imbalances.

American industries are shaken to their roots, and survival is a key issue for many firms. Lobbies of major industries are pressuring for some form of protection, the most publicized efforts of which represent the makers of automobiles and steel. The automobile industry is in the unprecedented position of having a foreign competitor that has gained the second largest share of the American market. Almost 25 percent of all cars sold are Japanese imports. In fact, the United States is the Japanese car makers' largest market, larger than its own. The steel industry has filed complaints with our Government about the foreign producer practice of dumping, apparently with justification, according to recent reports.

How and why an American share of international trade of 18 percent in 1950 dwindled to less than half that figure in 1980 is a subject best left to economists and industry experts.

In focusing on the fashion industry, the record is also discouraging, and the outlook grim. Using 1969 to 1979 as the base period, apparel imports increased 43 percent, and the trade record of shoes, a related product, had an increase of 486 percent. In other terms, the current yearly retail sales of foreign produced apparel are about $30 billion, approximately one of every three garments sold; with the percentage of foreign made shoes over 50 percent of units sold.

The dichotomy of what the Government should do about our current international trade vulnerability can make a logical case for both pros and cons of protectionism. The reality, however, is barring a catastrophic event or condition, we are committed to a "free" market, with some probability of minor adjustments to import terms.

The Government has attempted to alleviate the problem with no success:

- The GATT Agreement of 1979 has some value for international traders, but will probably have little influence in ameliorating trade imbalances.
- The Revitalization Act of 1976 to aid the shoe industry had modest initial impact, but the tide of imports have accelerated again in terms of both units and dollars.
- Grants to apparel trade unions to coordinate the efforts of labor and management to build a more productive and competitive industry are sound investments for the future.
- Orderly Marketing Agreements allow 6 percent increases of foreign imports in a market that has a 2 percent growth factor.

The Industry and Trade Administration of the Department of Commerce representatives are holding meetings with manufacturers, demonstrating the use of "tools" of Government, and encouraging broadened marketing horizons by exporting. The Administration recently established grants for studies to determine the feasibility of creating trading companies to ensure exporting on a constant and more intense scale. This idea was considered two years ago, but abandoned. Regardless of newer recommendations, it is questionable whether more liberal trading company guidelines could satisfy government and business.

Manufacturers in a highly competitive and opportunistic market are not prone to work within the framework of a consortium. If goverment-offered advantages far outweigh what could be achieved individually, perhaps there could be some producer compliance. But the probability is that Government will be unable or unwilling to offer inducements that manufacturers would consider as sufficient reason to be "married" to other firms.

The Webb-Pomerene Act of 1918 has been ineffective in attracting apparel producers to band together as international trade partners. It may well be that our geographic location and economic background mitigate against the concept of consortia, so successfully operated by Japanese trading companies and European banks.

In face of shrinking markets, many American apparel producers are faced with the alternatives of expansion or business demise.

Exporting is a way of extending a firm's market, well within the ability of most.

Unfamiliarity with the "hows" of exporting have created problems in the minds of those who have entertained the thought of using this marketing strategy. The oceans that separate us from most countries of the world look too formidable to bridge for those weaned on the domestic advantages of a large population, established marketing guidelines, proven garment specifications and colors, and fashion conscious consumers' willingness to indulge in the luxury of making apparel obsolete for the purpose of change. Marketing parochialism, however, is not confined to the fashion industry, less than 10 percent of all manufacturing entities are engaged in foreign trade.

For the most part, apparel manufacturer concerns about entering into international trade are unfounded. One of the most basic problems is that the vast majority of firms are small. They do not think in global terms because, like most other producers, there was never a compelling need to search for markets beyond national boundaries.

One of the peculiar income tax regulations requires reporting income earned overseas. For a small firm, this could be considered an inhibiting factor to personal investigation of foreign market opportunities, since employees assigned to some fertile markets would have to be paid several times the domestic pay scale to subsist.

Other problems are:

- Documentation requirements appear to be a mountain of red tape.
- International monetary values are confusing, particularly the subject of non-convertible currency.
- Differences in required size specifications and marketing techniques.
- Need for working capital to obtain a foreign market share.
- Fear that the only way to do business is by bribery.
- Inability to establish an export division.

Most of these problems can be "solved" by a Department of Commerce trade representative or export specialist (international shipper, banker, etc.).

There are six ways for American firms to export:

- International division
- Export subsidiary
- Export management company
- Webb-Pomerene Association
- Financial intermediary company

*Strategies and Tactics in Fashion Marketing*

- Market intelligence company.

The simplest method of exportation is through an international division which can consist of one person who concentrates on overseas sales. Naturally, this could suit the strategy of a small firm that has modest goals.

As a prudent business person, an apparel producer should consider the current record, the "starting line." Honesty dictates the conclusion that as exporters, "Our machinery is rusty and not hitting on all cylinders." Apparel exports are only 2 percent of total market shipments. However, the other side of the coin is, there is capability and potential, if the state of mind is to succeed—the same thinking demanded for success in any business—domestic or foreign.

The textile industry is a shining example of positive thinking. For several years, textile companies have been laying the groundwork for a sizable export business. In 1979, textile companies shipped a record $3.2 billion, up from $2.2 billion in 1978. This 45 percent increase was achieved by exporting yarn, fabric, and carpeting, products that have strong competition from foreign producers. The most optimistic note is the areas that purchased these products. Approximately half the goods were shipped to Canada and Europe. About 20 percent was to places like Hong Kong and Mexico. The remainder, 30 percent, was exported to customers in Asia, Africa, and Latin America.

This industry is embarked on a course to make deep inroads into foreign market with highly qualified credentials. The industry accounts for 20 percent of world production, an indication of capability, particularly in view of its having made considerable investment in the latest available technology, the most up-to-date machinery. In addition, textile executives recognize that consumers of many foreign countries have developed an appetite for American products and lifestyle, and have explored areas of greatest product receptivity.

A small size manufacturer might be prone to discount the textile market's record, and rebut it with: "Textile firms are large and have facilities and personnel beyond small business capability."

Here is a success story of a relatively small-size producer of boys' activewear. Robert Abels, the president of Scoreboard, a firm established in 1975, decided to build an export division into his operation. The decision was reached just nine months ago. His first step was to place an employee in charge of foreign sales. Both he and his export manager visited the Department of Commerce offices in Washington and New York City. After gathering information from government trade representatives, they requested inclusion in overseas bulletins the Department sends out regularly. With a list of foreign stores and buying offices, they were able to send out their own letters of introduction. These efforts yielded 200 inquiries.

As a supporting tactic, Abels arranged to show his line at regional markets and trade shows, which are frequented by many foreign buyers.

Without a foreign trip, with some investment of his time, and the full time concentration of one employee with no training in foreign selling, he was able to achieve foreign sales volume of 5 percent of his total year's shipments. He now plans to make foreign trade 15 to 20 percent of his yearly sales.

"Specifications, colors, and other regional requirements present no difficulty," he said. "As far as we are concerned, foreign stores and their buyers are no different from their American counterparts: they are professionals; they know what they want; they are willing to travel for what they need; and they speak the same language—English. I am considering a trip abroad, my first in business, to get deeper into the "water" and see some of the bases of operation firsthand."

"My advice to a newcomer is to visit the Industry and Trade people of the Department of Commerce immediately following a decision to "go" abroad."

It can be said with reasonable certainty, the vast majority of American fashion manufacturers are unaware of foreign market enthusiasm for our goods. They have heard of the successes of Levi Strauss and Blue Bell, but are too willing to ascribe them to bigness and the international trend for blue jeans. These factors are true, but not the complete story.

As an example of average market negativism, a committee of buyers from Japan tried to purchase American-made apparel for export during a visit to the Miami International Mart a year ago. Not one manufacturer or representative would take an order. The Japanese left empty-handed, bewildered by American manufacturer attitudes. At this time, manufacturer consensus is that exporting takes too much time, trouble, and knowledge.

No business activity is all roses. Garment specifications, colors, market timing, quantities and other conditions vary with market, without question. Documents, shipping terms, means of payment, and other arrangements must be handled. But, as noted, specialists can reduce these requirements to business as usual.

The present rate of exports, as noted, represents 2 percent of total apparel market shipments, and 5 percent of the textile industry figures, but they are bound to increase with appropriate interest and effort.

The subject of a devaluated dollar as it relates to international trading has not been discussed, even though it makes for more attractive current foreign purchase conditions.

The long-range view of exporting is that it widens marketing opportunities, including permanent relationships, organizational viability and stability.

## 20. UNDERSTANDING THE "JEAN PHENOMENON"

The blue jean's genesis and duration of success is a remarkable incident in the history of ready-to-wear. Although one can never predict the course of future fashions with any degree of certainty, the likelihood of a similar occurrence is not within the range of probability.

Manufacturers and retailers are realistic; the search for a fashion replacement, they recognize, is not a pragmatic expectation. But, the jean story offers lessons in consumer behavior and fashion marketing principles that will be considered in their future planning.

When Levi Straus died in 1902, he had no reason to suspect that he had created a pant that would become the most important fashion in the world. His motivation was to make trousers for miners that would withstand the rigors of gold mining. Certainly, he never conceived that his sturdy, serviceable jean would be embraced by well-heeled women in the 1930's during vacations on dude ranches; would become the uniform of the disillusioned and the disenfranchised during the 1960's; and that it would carry famous designer names in the 1970's and 1980's.

The jean has penetrated every market segment—men, women, children, and even large-sizes. And one of the remarkable factors is that, although there are variations in styling—slim, hip-huggers, harem silhouette, among other details—the fabric (in different weights) remains the same, the blue color is of predominant importance, and the garment reflects the same look as originally conceived. In some cases, even simulation of the handiwork of the harness which Levi Straus employed by featuring metal rivets remains.

In the classic evolution of fashion, the blue jean should have "died" from customer boredom at the end of the 1960's. It should have become the sole domain of manufacturers of work clothes, and relegated to the less productive sales areas of retail stores. But 20 years after its rise to an almost all-pervasive popularity, T.V. commercials feature more than a fair share of women, men and children dancing in a manner that is characterized in industry circles as salacious, sometimes in bad taste, even "immoral." But customers, it appears, listen to a different "drummer." If customers are offended, it is not reflected in retail sales—not yet.

The aftermath of commercial success motivates research concentration on the factors that contributed to, or directly affected, a product's importance. In the case of blue jeans, the confluence of events that led to this international importance has been well-documented, principally by Charles Reich in his "The Greening of America." Our focus is the identification of some of the major considerations that marketers will weigh and possibly implement as part of their future marketing strategies—based on the blue jean experience.

## A Love-Hate Attitude

The following are factors which have contributed to the "jean phenomenon:"

*Influence of Brand Names*—During the past 20 years, there has been continuous dialogue concerning the importance of branding. Manufacturers, in most instances, question the high cost and their ability to attain a brand name position. Retailers often express a love-hate attitude. Well accepted brands offer the advantages of easier selling and ample markup. However, over-branding can have a stifling effect on fashion newness and adequate style assortment.

Objectively, quality variances from one jean to another do not justify price differences—not by far. The retail price of one of the oldest jean manufacturers is $15, not significantly higher than it was 15 years ago. On the other hand, "johnny-come-lately's" to the business are able to distribute their designer-label styles to sell successfully from $30 to $50.

The answer points to a critical relationship between price and manufacturer name: the brand. This is no attempt to denigrate the value of fit, which is featured by some manufacturers. But, in the main, jean purchases are strongly influenced by a search for status. A well-identified designer name on the backside connotes a status symbol.

The theory is hardly new. The La Coste alligator shirt success story predates the importance of designer-name jeans. What is novel is the profusion of jean brands, the number of success stories based on branding, and the wide acceptance of the higher prices in a market with ample supply of comparable lower-priced versions.

In this new brand-name selling environment, the manufacturer's primary consideration is to obtain the right to use a well-known designer's name. The retailer's main concern is to stock brand name merchandise in certain classifications that offer status appeal.

*Power of Advertising*—Advertising is obviously related to branding. An average apparel manufacturer spends less than one percent of net sales for sales promotion; a retailer budgets between three to four percent.

Jean selling is a breakthrough in fashion marketing. It represents the first broadside successful manufacturer effort to use T.V. as a major advertising medium. Where would the Gloria Vanderbilt jean be without the influence of the "tube?"

Telecommunication is in its infancy, but there is no doubt that cable T.V. will soon feature fashions as frequently as most other products. Branding will become wider in scope with the increased opportunities of area broadcasts, lowered T.V. costs and growing consumer interest in fashion shows.

*The Great Population Shift*—The census of 1980 reveals that the area in which the jean originated is now the fastest growing part of the nation. The subcultural influences of the Sun Belt, the South, the Southwest and the Far West are beginning to exert their influence on national fashion. New York based firms will be less likely to impress their fashion concepts on the rest of the country. Sun-Belt regions increasingly will demand fashions that have their subcultural values included.

## Jeans and Future Fashion

What are apparel manufacturers going to do to accommodate the "Urban Cowboy" or "Cowgirl" who wears $700 boots; a $400 animal skin shirt; a $500 silver belt; a $200 Stetson hat and a *pressed* pair of blue jeans that is only dry cleaned, never washed? High style, it is true. Perhaps this is limited evidence of what may become a broader trend, and perhaps a far-fetched relationship between the jean and future fashion.

Manufacturers must develop styling appropriate in silhouette, color, fabric and detail for Sun-Belt wear. Retailers must keep an alert eye on Sun-Belt fashions lest there be another "jean" type development on the horizon. And additionally, as previously reported, large-scale retailers will establish more branches in the Sun-Belt region.

*"Breaking Down the Walls"*—One of the more difficult aspects of fashion marketing is to produce, or retail, garments for both adults and children. Different buyers, different departments and different store merchandising divisions have erected barriers for manufacturers who tried to capitalize on the importance of their adult fashions by extending them into children's wear. The children's buyer was prone to stay with traditional manufacturers of children's wear.

The jean has been instrumental in reducing the barriers between retail merchandise classifications. The past practice of making different types of apparel for varying age groups is an outgrowth of American industry dedication to specialization, a situation that does not exist in many other countries. For example, Japanese apparel firms design merchandise for both adult and youth consumption.

The jean has proven the American manufacturers' ability to make some styles in different size ranges for both sexes, and for adults as well as children. The result is a broadening of marketing opportunities for both manufacturers and retailers.

The jean phenomenon demonstrates that in the 1980's consumers seek apparel that makes a statement; intrinsic value has a diminished importance compared with social acceptance.

The jean started with the emulation of cowboy garb, progressed to a uniform to evidence discontent and anti-establishment feeling, and finally, to a status symbol. The jean epitomizes the "democratization" of fashion—availability to one and all.

## 21. PRESIDENT REAGAN'S OPTIONS TO AID BUSINESS: AN INTERPRETATION

Whether or not the Reagan administration declares a national economic emergency, it is certain that a broadside attack will be mounted against a montage of bleak conditions that include double-digit inflation; unprecedented high prime interest rates; a 39 cent dollar compared to 1967; persistent high unemployment; and industries vital to our economy shaken to their very foundations. Another certainty is that the new president will not lack advice. Staff executives, the media, and economists will be profuse in their assessments and suggested cures, which promise to be more numerous than the problems. Unfortunately, selection of effective economic alternatives is a vexing problem. Tinkering with economic forces or the application of a textbook theory, more often than not, causes the domino effect of setting in motion a series of unforeseen events that compound the original problem. Economics, at best, is a social science which has precision after the fact.

It is safe to say that the Administration will not resort, in any significant degree, to the safest but least effective ploy of presidential "jawboning," a technique that has been used far too often in the recent past. Our problems are too critical and protracted to depend upon this stalling-for-time tactic, hoping that an equilibrium of demand and supply will come about through the natural forces of economic evolution.

It will take at least six months to assess the direction and vigor of the Administration's efforts to ameliorate or revise the course of our impacted woes. The hope is that steps within the philosophy of conservatism will create clarity out of present confusion. Perhaps the new President, reputed to be more pragmatic than scholarly, will translate the complexities of the issues we face into simple terms and take effective "arms" against them.

Governor Reagan as a presidential candidate expressed concern for reasons numerous American products, once considered among the world's best, are now in the also-ran category of international trade, and even worse, in second, or no place, in our domestic market. He and his advisors are well aware of the plight of producers of automobiles, steel, textiles, clothing, shoes, television sets, cameras, sewing machines, ad infinitum. Product market share losses must be, in large part, symptomatic of our economic state.

Parenthetically, it is ironic that industries that decry government business regulations are pressing for its support. In truth, a political system is fundamentally an economic entity, and it is logical for government to be involved in how business is conducted and how its efforts assist citizens to achieve and maintain a standard of living. On the other hand, regulations can be inhibitive and sap business vitality. But whether there is excessive government business intrusion, the *laissez-faire* theory—that government and business are and should remain two separate entities—has not been practiced in the United States since the Civil War.

When President Reagan focuses his sights on the subject of aid to business, it will be surprising if he does not select the automobile industry as a first priority. This business sector is vital to our economic well-being; it accounts for approximately one-fifth of our gross national product and employs almost one-sixth of our workers. In addition, it is a source of equipment required for national defense. How Detroit fares could determine our future economic path. Steps that lead to the bellwether industry's improvement could be a matrix for other businesses to follow.

From the pinnacle of international and domestic success, the automobile business plunged into a state of crisis. The big three, General Motors, Ford and Chrysler, experienced huge losses in 1980, collectively about $4 billion, with General Motors in the red for the first time since 1921. The hardest hit, Chrysler, is teetering on the brink of bankruptcy. In its weakness, the industry is lobbying for protection from foreign producers, particularly Japanese automakers. As further signs of weakness, Ford is reported to be negotiating with Toyo Kogyo Co., Japan's third-largest automaker, to produce at least 150,000 sub-compact cars annually; and a circumstance beyond comprehension only a few years ago, UAW's president visited Japan to influence its automotive industry to locate factories in the United States.

It is generally conceded that the confluence of self-destructive marketing, a depressed economy, the oil shortage, and superior foreign products brought about the industry's market share loss.

Government steps to aid the automobile industry will be demanded by other industries, it is certain. That the Japanese automakers have captured almost 25 percent of our market is a sad state of affairs, but the shoe industry, for example, has suffered a market share loss of 50 percent to foreign countries. And regardless of the level of proposed government aid, there will be dissidents who will claim support given to the private sector is a reward for poor management. They will claim additionally that government help proliferates mediocrity and therefore abets marginal firms' efforts to pay low-scale wages, encourages higher consumer prices, and finally, lowers the standard of living.

Industry's rebuttal for the decreasing importance of our products includes two arguments: one, the guidelines of international trade favor foreign producers; and two, because of our wealth and population size, we are a fertile market target for most trading countries. Clearly, every country enjoys some comparative advantage, such as location, cheap labor pool, or natural resources, which it exploits by producing goods that are better or cheaper than those of countries they select for exportation. And conversely, a country imports products from countries that make them better or more economically. Trade inequities, however, develop when a government furnishes incentives for its industries that allow products to be exported that reflect "manufactured" comparative advantages to the detriment of the producers of importing countries. This aggressive international trading scheme is often in tandem with still another tack, regulations that make its domestic market unprofitable for foreign producers. Industry alleges Japan is guilty on both counts.

The United States in its state of industrial and technological leadership was generous in granting trading terms favorable to other nations. The motivation, in honesty, was not completely ingenuous. It is long since when we had natural resource self-sufficiency; currently we have sufficient supply of the four of 24 required to maintain our industrial complex. Another compelling reason for our generosity is international trade has a strong relationship to détente or entente with other nations. We need amicable relations, even at the cost of granting concessions to the disadvantage of industry.

Setting up trade barriers is a disasterous route that could rupture our relationship with both friends and foes and tend to isolate us from the rest of the world. We simply cannot take unilateral action to change trading agreements, even if they are unfair. The perplexity of our position is that, regardless of how deeply some industries are hurting, our trade representatives will be forced to tread cautiously in their negotiations with other nations. Government will be forced to extend its greatest effort to effect business relief by concentrating on internal measures.

In the final analysis, it is industry's onus to find the path to market product importance by imposing stricter quality control techniques and the use of latest technological developments. It is Government's responsibility to create a climate in which profitability is obtainable and costly regulations are not imposed capriciously.

Within the range of options, the following could receive Presidential consideration to alleviate the automobile industry's plight in particular and business in general:

1. Liberalize the Webb-Pomerene Act of 1918, which could provide a way to establish industrial consortia to combat the advantages of foreign trading companies. (An amalgamation of industrial resources, technology, and capital could be a hard-to-beat combine.)
2. Establish a government/industry automotive research team to develop improvements through technology. (A bill has been introduced in Congress for the purpose, with each putting up half the cash required.)
3. Extend liberal commodity tax rebates on exported products (an incentive for profit and product improvement).
4. Establish a climate of cooperation. Government has been considered a business adversary far too long. (It would be well to study the Japanese government/industry relationship.)
5. Reduce corporate taxes. (A Reagan promise.)
6. Liberalize research and development expense tax allowances (an encouragement for product improvement).
7. Speed up the depreciation period for tax writeoffs on new plants and equipment (a reform on the President's list of aid to business measures).
8. Provide investment capital at low interest rates. Whether this is in accordance with international agreements, other trading nations provide this advantage (a considerable saving in a time of high cost of money).
9. Appoint trade representatives with disregard for political affiliation. Representatives should have a background of business success, and optimally, a knowledge of the marketing of products under negotiations. (The use of politicians is a luxury we can no longer afford.)
10. Negotiate trade agreements on realistic terms. Orderly Marketing Agreements, as noted, have, in too many instances, worked to the disadvantage of depressing industries. (We should be generous but not profligate.)

Most wish the President success in his efforts to meet the critical challenges of the 1980's. For the sake of all Americans, after the rice is out of his hair and the honeymoon is over, it is hoped that most are pleased with the "marriage" ceremony of January 20, 1981.

## 22. THE MATURATION OF BRANCH STORES

Since the "Retail Revolution" of the 1950's, large scale retailers have continued to open new "branches" (A branch is a unit of a main store; a chain does not have a main store.) to increase their share of targeted markets. Over the years, branch store operations of depart-

*Trends*

ment stores and specialty stores assumed greater volume importance than "parent" or downtown stores. Chain stores also increased their number of units in response to growing retail markets and the shifting location of retail markets. More became better.

The proliferation of units and increased volume, however, have not always assured success. In fact, recent retail failures are unparalleled, as witnessed by the demise of W.T. Grant and Interstate Department Stores; the closing of the Franklin Simon chain; and the shutdown of 14 Korvette units.

Branch operations, once the *sine qua non* of department and specialty store viability, now are often examples of retail anomalies. Stern's, formerly of New York, operates without its original anchor store. Carter, Hawley Hale closed down its Bergdorf-Goodman branch in White Plains, N.Y., and is replacing it with a Nieman-Marcus branch; and the Hempstead, L.I., N.Y. branch of Abraham and Straus, once considered a premier satellite unit, is now in danger of being closed.

There is no question but that the uncontrollable factors of urban and suburban decay, population shifts, management changes, energy shortage, inflation, and intense competition have taken their toll. On the other hand, even in a milieu of the most repeated retail failures—New York City—there are examples of retail success: the well-publicized "change-arounds" of R.H. Macy and Bloomingdales.

Perhaps the current retail environment is analogous to a product's life cycle that includes a stage of maturity, when competition becomes keen and an organization is faced with three alternatives: update the product, abandon the product, or accept a more limited share of a declining market. The first alternative often requires some combination of imagination, careful planning, and additional investment.

Since department stores were in the vanguard of the movement to "branching," it is reasonable to assume that they could be the bellwether for branch directions in the 1980's. Accordingly, we interviewed a vice-president of a nationally known, New York based department store chain, with more than 30 years of branch store operation experience.

The response to the query, "What are your organization's plans for additional branches in the 1980's?", proved that considerable analysis had been given to the subject, and that their plans are very much in place.

"Our approach is two-pronged; one, from a conglomerate viewpoint, and two, from the vantage of our regional corporations, each of which operates a main store and branches within defined trading areas. Therefore, the direction of the total corporation is to expand. Obviously, like most large-scale retail organizations, we have our

*Strategies and Tactics in Fashion Marketing*

sights set on areas within the fastest growing section of the country—the Sun-Belt.

"Our branch store experience dictates that the pattern of operation must be influenced by the conditions of a continued population growth, reasonable quantitative and qualitative levels of competition, favorable consumer identification of our retail image and our established retail mix. In other words, our philosophy can be characterized as being selective.

"Regional corporation expansion opportunities will be scrutinized even more closely, and we will exercise a higher degree of selectivity because most established trading areas have been well-exploited, with limited opportunities to create new, viable marketplaces. We feel there is greater opportunity in enhancing our present ownership, by improving current operations: refurbishing interiors, taking a more precise fix on our customer needs, and raising the quality of our services and communications.

"Although the New York area cannot be considered a microcosm, the fact is that this region's main store and branches contribute a major volume share to our corporate volume, and, to a large degree, constitute a pace-setting operation for the rest of the chain. What happens in New York could be experienced in other regions later. Therefore, our New York background must be the basis of our thinking.

"For a period of 25 years, we were able to place a protractor over our main store location, draw a line in any direction up to 50 miles, and come up with a suitable branch store site. Expansion was reasonable, continuous, and profitable. But what happened? Every one of our branches is now surrounded by every type of retailer, including factory outlets and other pipe rack operations. Competition has become all-pervasive, a retail condition for most well-established branch store operations in major trading areas.

"The additional conditions of an energy shortage, continuing inflation, and shopping center deterioration are additional important negative factors in considering expansion. Whether these counter-currents will be reversed is debatable, but the facts are they are very much a part of retail life and must be faced.

"An affirmative note for some suburban operations is that the population flow to the "edge" of suburbia has slowed down considerably. The movement to far-out places no longer offers the advantages of a lower cost home and a unique lifestyle. The result, therefore, is that suburban area land gaps are being filled in by newcomers and providing additional potential consumers.

"To summarize our approach to expansion in regional markets in which we are currently operating, we will weigh the expansion feasibility only if unusual circumstances can lead to a satisfactory return on investment, and also point to our ability to "control" a market share in a market that is demographically and psychographically in tune with our corporate objectives."

We pointed out that interior store improvement may have only limited effect in improving consumer patronage motives. Consumers, it was noted, like to shop where they are comfortable, but today's economic pressures are causing a deep concern to obtain maximum value, and it is only product that can reflect intrinsic value. "How", it was asked, "do you outflank your competition by offering greater value?"

"That," responded the retailer, "is a good question."

"Within the condition of intense competition, we simply cannot sell the same goods as low-overhead operators. After all, retail prices must reflect the cost of doing business, and ours include the costs of a full service department store. Therefore, we must give the type of service the customer pays for and deserves, and additionally offer merchandise that is not 'footballed'.

"Our stock must be confined to customer identified brands known for quality and fashion-rightness. In this effort we will feature designer name brands, with strong stock representation at moderate to better price levels. Every effort will be made to minimize our carrying the same merchandise as competitors, particularly those we equate as unfair competitors. The criteria we have set up for manufacturers will be enforced rigidly, and will include: merchandise suitability for our customers, proper delivery, and under what conditions merchandise is available to ultimate consumers."

As a corollary to merchandise procurement, we asked: "To what degree will you develop exclusive merchandise through specification merchandising?"

"Specification merchandising is a highly desired practice in a competitive market," said the retail executive. "We do it to a limited degree, and it may have greater interest for us in the future, but we recognize an inherent weakness in our organization. Our average buyer is not sufficiently experienced to undertake the responsibilities of a sophisticated method of merchandise procurement. Our buying staff turnover is too rapid to permit our staff to accumulate the experience and confidence to exercise technique of "producing" goods and facing the contingency of big mistakes. Perhaps we will consider using our resident buying-office for the purpose. In this way, our buyers could work with buying office personnel of extended tenure and gain the benefit of consensus decisions. However, it is a decision that is being held in abeyance at the time."

And finally, we asked the predictable, "Aside from the problems discussed, what are the new or recurring problems of branch store management?"

"Communication between the personnel of parent and branch stores continues to plague us. How to establish a two-way communication, how to train young executives to set priorities in order of merchandising importance, and how to ensure proper follow-through on merchandising activities still elude us.

"Branch store personnel turnover is far too rapid for management efficiency. It must be realized that branch store junior executives are, by far, in temporary positions, those that lead to permanent executive placement. Every manager is impatient for promotion, an understandable attitude.

"Branch store pilferage has increased and is now on a par with main store losses.

"Despite experience and carefully accumulated data, the demographic and psychographic differences from store to store make it difficult to stock merchandise that responds specifically to the customer profiles of particular stores. The problem is most acute in the fashion merchandising area.

"In general, the questions of what is the most appropriate branch store size, what merchandise classifications bear greatest importance, and what is the best method of operation, remain to be solved.

"One of the newer problems is suburban decay. It is sad to see the deterioration that has taken place in so many shopping centers.

"In the 1950's and 1960's, we identified certain classifications as having suburban importance, such as: car coats, sweaters, jackets, slacks, and other articles of apparel that were interpreted as having importance for a casual lifestyle. But today, with women 41.7 percent of the work force, it is necessary to change our ideas about merchandise mix importance. If females are, and becoming to a greater degree, executives, then they must be given greater credence than by showing them on T.V. in three-piece suits reading the *Wall Street Journal.*

"Executives need traveling robes, traveling clocks, attache cases, traveling bags, and all the accoutrements of executive life. Do branch stores cater to these needs? Will it take new arrangement of merchandise in branches already pressed for space? Will branches set up merchandise by lifestyle for the convenience of time-pressed career women?

"Branch stores have grown like Topsey; there is no uniformity in size, design, merchandising, and operation. It is a certainty that future success will demand more than a desirable location and the opportunity for volume."

As a *post mortem* over a cup of coffee, the following was asked, "What are your thoughts about telecommunication and the computer as part of retail expansion in the 1980's?"

"Sears Roebuck has already taken a step that may be in that direction. They are in partnership for the development of a COMSAT system. So far, the government has not been asked for or given permission to use the development to broadcast catalogue information. Certainly, technological availabilities are a wave of the future and could well make inroads into branch store importance. In the meantime, catalogue stores are in the retail environment in tremendous numbers, and mail and telephone merchandising are part of the merchandising plans of every retailer—conventional and non-conventional."

Retailing is the largest segment of our economy, and highly responsive to new environmental conditions. It will be interesting to track the direction of an important component of retailing during the 1980's—branch stores. The maturation of branch stores is here: 30 years of age is when one joins the establishment.

## 23. FASHION MARKETING IMPLICATIONS OF THE 1980 CENSUS

Although the accuracy of the 1980 census has been challenged, principally by states that stand to lose national government largess and congressional representation, the relevant dimension of the figures are sufficiently clear-cut for apparel producers and retailers to use them as a base to project plans for organizational growth and profitability in the 1980's. From the outset, marketers will be most concerned with four demographic factors: population size, income, population location, and the size and purchasing power of age groups. But even with statistics favorable to increased marketing opportunities, apparel producers, in particular, will not be prone to go off the deep end in their plans for the early 1980's. The business climate is too overcast with clouds of economic uncertainty: unprecedented high cost of money, consumers under pressure to maintain a standard of living, and intense foreign market competition that is likely to increase with anticipated agreements with China and other countries entering the industrial age. But a comparison of the statistics of 1970 and 1980 do point to an atmosphere that could be conducive to business growth.

In general, the census shows dramatic changes over the decade, most notably an increased population whose median age is somewhat older, somewhat more prosperous, and increasingly disposed to living in the Sun Belt.

As a primary consideration, our population grew, but at what rate is debatable. However, it is reasonable to assume the 1980 population figure as approximately 230 million, based on an adjusted total of 226 million plus probable unregistered alien residents and other uncounted persons. The growth factor ranges from 9 to 11 percent, depending upon the base figure used. Although the rate of growth was the second slowest in history, when related to more people in higher income brackets, they add up to reasons for optimism, since approximately 10 percent of disposable income is spent on apparel.

Although population growth is an indication of increased opportunity, there is need to qualify or "polish" the figure by analyzing market segments, identifying location and importance of regional markets. Apparel demand to a large degree is predicated on merchandise's relationship to climatic conditions and regional standards.

Parenthetically, from the time our nation was founded, population movement has been amazing. Americans are among the most nomadic people in the world, approximately 25 percent of all Americans change their addresses each year. In the main, however, the migration is largely within the same county and/or state.

Three major population shifts during the 20th century have caused dramatic changes in retail institutions, and the strategies of fashion marketers.

In 1920 the rural population started to move to urban areas in considerable numbers. In that year the farm population was 30 percent, a figure that has dwindled to 4 percent. Population compression laid the groundwork for the birth of modern ready-to-wear. Increased city population led to groups that tended to share similar views, one of which was appropriate apparel for cosmopolitan attire. In due course, mass production has attained mass acceptance. As a consequence, the dress business entered the arena of big business, and chain stores took advantage of their market-based (New York) home office location by feeding their stores dress styles as they came off the production line. Department stores recognized their relative weakness as compared to chains and went after the dress business with serious intent. Although it took a confluence of events for ready-to-wear's birth and growth, the population shift created the necessary environment.

The second migration started immediately following World War II, the exodus from the cities to the green grass of suburbia. This movement influenced apparel producers to go more casual in styling. And of greater significance, it was the catalyst for the "Retail Revolution"—a radical change in our retail distribution system. Chains extended their retail units, department and specialty store organizations went from single locations to multi-unit operations, and discount stores assumed importance. The expansion included the trend of some parochial operations going national. The population distribution of this migration resulted in 40 percent of all Americans now residing in suburban areas, 33 percent in rural areas, and the remainder 27 percent in central cities. Apparel producers and retailers all more or less properly positioned to accommodate this population distribution, although many retailers are concerned with branch store location deterioration and unexpected intense competition.

The current and continuing movement to the Sun Belt has held the attention of fashion marketers for some time. Regional manufacturers have been in a position to distribute styles of regional importance, and retail organizations have erected branch stores in some newly developed trading areas. But the concentration on Sun Belt opportunities is in its infancy, the full impact of population change and marketing response to it is still in its formative stages.

National organizations are taking a long, hard look at demographics and calling upon their past experience for organizational expansion. It is reasonable and good marketing to learn from past mistakes. Here are a few highlights that are being studied. The West and the South are now 50 percent of the total population of the country. Considered as one unit, California, Texas, and Florida had a growth of 42 percent during the decade and now total 46 million people—approximately 20 percent of the total population.

There can be no doubt that major apparel producers and retailers are poised to "follow the sun." From the manufacturer's vantage point, lines can no longer concentrate on what is appropriate for temperate climate wear with some added sun colors for warm weather regions. Major markets require line concentration on their climatic conditions, regional standards and/or lifestyles. Migrants to the Sun Belt, it will have to be realized, shuck the raiment of their former areas of residency in favor of lighter weight, brighter colored, and more casual apparel. Lines for every season will be required to include Sun-Belt styles, a factor that will cause extended merchandise line assortments. Failure to concentrate on regional demands will open the door for local manufacturers who can offer the advantages of appropriate merchandise, faster delivery, and personal relationships.

Retailers have three alternatives: *concentrate on mailing catalogs to attract business, open catalog stores,* or *establish branch stores.* If the last alternative is selected, it is certain plans will be formulated after deliberation of:

- Past expansion experience
- Identifiable regional demographic and psychographic factors
- High cost of money
- Probable future competition
- Retail mix

*Strategies and Tactics in Fashion Marketing*

- Store size

As a fundamental marketing factor, marketers will seek groups that have sufficient wherewithal and willingness to spend it. Census figures in this regard are deceptive. Approximately 40 million people have an income of $15,000 or over, about 16 to 18 percent of the population. This record would seem to indicate that the nation is enjoying prosperity. The downside is that inflation has substantially lowered the purchasing power of the dollar, wiping out real income gain of most of the population. In the final analysis, however, the proportion of Americans living below the poverty level has been lowered, not that a substantial group of poverty-stricken people do not exist, the exact figure of which has never been determined. The upside of increased income is it tends to influence customers to trade up and enjoy newly attained income level status, even when disposable and discretionary incomes have limited purchasing power. The motivation of self-fulfillment is a strong pressure. But how retirees to the Sun Belt are reacting to inflation is a subject that requires research of characteristics of potential customers in particular trading areas.

The size and purchasing power of age groups are significant marketing concerns. Assortment of need is strongly related to lifecycle stage—different ages cause different needs and product preferences. For the second time in history the decennial census will show the median age of the U. S. population to be over 30 years; the first time was in 1950 before the postwar surge in births began to affect the nation's age distribution. There are now proportionately fewer people under age 20 than in 1970, many more at ages 20 to 34 and at all older ages except 45 to 54. A developing phenomenon is that persons 65 and older will outnumber teenagers within a few years.

**Total Population By Age**

| Percent by Age | 1970 | 1980 |
| --- | --- | --- |
| Under 5 | 8.4% | 7.2% |
| 5–9 | 9.8 | 7.3 |
| 10–14 | 10.2 | 8.0 |
| 15–19 | 9.4 | 9.3 |
| 20–24 | 8.1 | 9.4 |
| 25–34 | 12.3 | 16.3 |
| 35–44 | 11.4 | 11.6 |
| 45–54 | 11.4 | 10.2 |
| 55–64 | 9.1 | 9.5 |
| 65 and older | 9.9 | 11.2 |

A maturing population will cause pockets of dislocation in the fashion industry (e.g., teenage manufacturers), but it is a favorable marketing value for most, more people in maturity equate as a market of higher income consumers. Marketers, therefore, will segment population by age groups within regions and trading areas. Plans will reflect anticipated consumer groups: *frequency of purchases, desired price ranges and zones,* and *styling.* In Sun-Belt regions, *age delineation* is of paramount importance because of concentrated groups of senior citizens.

In summary, the census of 1980 proves dramatic changes during the decade. However, fashion marketing will accommodate the changes just as it always has. Sensitivity to influences and responsive action are inherent industry characteristics.

# About the Author

Sidney Packard's marketing career is long and varied. In business, he held executive positions or ownership of firms in the fields of retailing, resident buying, manufacturing, and consulting.

His academic activities include: many years with the Fashion Institute of Technology, where he developed the curriculum and coordinated the program of B.S. in Textile and Apparel Marketing; lectured for Cornell University School of Labor and Industrial Relations; led seminars for educational institutions, government, and industry; structured the Fashion Marketing program of Fu Jen University of Taiwan; conducted seminars for Asahi Chemical Company marketing groups in Tokyo, Japan; authorship of text books on various aspects of fashion marketing.

He is currently marketing consultant for *Knitting Times* and *Apparel World* and monthly columnist; a director of Fashion Education Consultants; adjunct professor of marketing at Florida Atlantic University (Boca Raton, Florida), and business analyst of the Small Business Development Center (F.A.U.).